D0517942

COMMON CORE
English Language Arts

in a PLC at Work™

LEADER'S GUIDE

DOUGLAS FISHER
NANCY FREY
CYNTHIA L. ULINE
Foreword by Richard DuFour

A Joint Publication With

INTERNATIONAL
Reading
Association

555 North Morton Street
Bloomington, IN 47404
800.733.6786 (toll free) / 812.336.7700
FAX: 812.336.7790

email: info@solution-tree.com
solution-tree.com

Visit **go.solution-tree.com/commoncore** to download the reproducibles in this book.

Printed in the United States of America

17 16 15 14 13   1 2 3 4 5

IRA Stock No. 9246

Library of Congress Cataloging-in-Publication Data

Fisher, Douglas, 1965-

  Common core English language arts in a PLC at work, leader's guide / Douglas Fisher, Nancy Frey, Cynthia L. Uline ; foreword by Richard DuFour.

      pages cm

  Includes bibliographical references and index.

  ISBN 978-1-936764-13-6 (perfect bound) 1. Language arts--Standards--United States. 2. Language arts--Curricula--United States. 3. Professional learning communities. I. Frey, Nancy, 1959- II. Uline, Cynthia L. III. Title.

  LB1576.F4425 2013

  372.6--dc23

                          2012051440

Solution Tree
Jeffrey C. Jones, CEO
Edmund M. Ackerman, President

Solution Tree Press
President: Douglas M. Rife
Publisher: Robert D. Clouse
Editorial Director: Lesley Bolton
Managing Production Editor: Caroline Wise
Senior Production Editor: Joan Irwin
Copy Editor: Sarah Payne-Mills
Proofreader: Elisabeth Abrams
Cover and Text Designer: Jenn Taylor

TABLE OF CONTENTS

ABOUT THE AUTHORS

Douglas Fisher, PhD, is a professor of educational leadership at San Diego State University and a teacher leader at Health Sciences High and Middle College. He teaches courses in instructional improvement. As a classroom teacher, Fisher focuses on English language arts instruction. He also serves as the literacy instructional advisor to the Chula Vista Elementary School District.

Fisher received an International Reading Association Celebrate Literacy Award for his work on literacy leadership and was elected to the board of directors in 2012. For his work as codirector of the City Heights Professional Development Schools, Fisher received the Christa McAuliffe Award. He was corecipient of the Farmer Award for excellence in writing from the National Council of Teachers of English for the article "Using Graphic Novels, Anime, and the Internet in an Urban High School," published in the *English Journal*.

Fisher has written numerous articles on reading and literacy, differentiated instruction, and curriculum design. He is the author of numerous books, including *In a Reading State of Mind*, *Checking for Understanding*, *Better Learning Through Structured Teaching*, *Text Complexity*, *Literacy 2.0*, *Teaching Students to Read Like Detectives*, *Implementing RTI With English Learners*, and *The School Leader's Guide to English Learners*.

He earned a bachelor's degree in communication, a master's degree in public health education, and a doctoral degree in multicultural education. Fisher completed post-doctoral study at the National Association of State Boards of Education focused on standards-based reforms.

Nancy Frey, PhD, is a professor of literacy in the School of Teacher Education at San Diego State University. Through the university's teacher-credentialing and reading specialist programs, she teaches courses on elementary and secondary reading instruction and literacy in content areas, classroom management, and supporting students with diverse learning needs. Frey also serves as a teacher leader at Health Sciences High and Middle College in San Diego. She was a board member of the California Reading Association and is a credentialed special educator, reading specialist, and administrator in California.

Before joining the university faculty, Frey was a public school teacher in Florida. She worked at the state level for the Florida Inclusion Network helping districts design systems for supporting students with disabilities in general education classrooms.

She is the recipient of the 2008 Early Career Achievement Award from the National Reading Conference and the Christa McAuliffe Award for excellence in teacher education from the American Association of State Colleges and Universities. She was corecipient of the Farmer Award for excellence in writing from the National Council of Teachers of English for the article "Using Graphic Novels, Anime, and the Internet in an Urban High School" published in the *English Journal*.

Frey is the author of numerous books, including *The Formative Assessment Action Plan, Productive Group Work, Teaching Students to Read Like Detectives, Content-Area Conversations, Literacy 2.0, Teaching Students to Read Like Detectives, Implementing RTI With English Learners*, and *The School Leader's Guide to English Learners*. She has written articles for *The Reading Teacher, Journal of Adolescent and Adult Literacy, English Journal, Voices From the Middle, Middle School Journal, Remedial and Special Education*, and *Educational Leadership*.

Cynthia L. Uline, PhD, is a professor of educational leadership at San Diego State University. She previously served as an assistant and associate professor of educational administration at The Ohio State University from 1995 to 2005. Uline codirects San Diego State's doctoral program in educational leadership and serves as executive director of the National Center for the 21st Century Schoolhouse. The center supports the planning and design of learner-centered schools through communication, research, and training.

Uline's research explores the influence of built learning environments on students' learning, as well as the role educational leaders, teachers, and the community play in shaping these learning spaces. Other areas of research include school leadership for learning and school reform and improvement.

She has written articles for *Educational Administration Quarterly*, *Journal of Educational Administration*, *Teachers College Record*, *Journal of School Leadership*, *Journal of Education for Students Placed at Risk*, *Theory Into Practice*, *Journal of Research and Development in Education*, and *International Journal of Leadership in Education*. She has coauthored several books, including *Building a Professional Community* and *Teaching Practices From America's Best Urban Schools*.

To book Douglas Fisher, Nancy Frey, or Cynthia L. Uline for professional development, contact pd@solution-tree.com.

FOREWORD

The adoption of the Common Core State Standards (CCSS) offers educators both an opportunity and a challenge. For the first time, the United States has acknowledged that in a global society the knowledge and skills students require are not limited to the boundaries of their state. For the first time, the United States has taken meaningful steps to articulate the essential learnings for all students whether they live in New York or New Mexico. A key aspect of effective teaching is that the teacher knows exactly what students must learn, and the Common Core State Standards represent a coordinated effort to help educators address that issue in a consistent and coherent way.

But this is not the first attempt to improve schools by adopting a new curriculum. The launching of Sputnik led to a spate of reforms in the 1960s to increase the rigor of curricula, particularly in mathematics and science. *A Nation at Risk* in 1983 led to over three hundred state and national commissions examining ways to improve schooling. Strengthening curriculum was one of the most common recommendations to save U.S. schools from "a rising tide of mediocrity." The adoption of curriculum standards in core subject areas by each state in the late 1980s and 1990s represents yet another attempt to strengthen schools through curriculum reform.

Thus, history demonstrates that having a nation, state, or district adopt a new curriculum does not guarantee that students will achieve at higher levels. Writing a new curriculum is relatively easy. Effectively implementing the new curriculum in all classrooms is incredibly difficult. Those who examine the Common Core from a cynical perspective are likely to respond to the initiative with a dismissive "this-too-shall-pass" reaction.

If educators are to overcome the formidable challenge of implementing the CCSS in a way that leads to higher levels of student learning, they will need help in two critical areas. The first is a deep understanding of the content of the standards and what they require of students. The second is a clarity regarding an effective implementation process that is vital to substantive change in schools.

As educators grapple with these challenges, scores of books are being written to support their efforts. Some books are intended to offer deeper insights into the standards themselves. These books offer helpful information about the nature of the standards and clarify how those standards translate into the specific knowledge and skills all students must acquire. Other books attempt to provide suggestions regarding a change process that will help educators move the Common Core from words in a document to a driving force in the classroom.

Common Core English Language Arts in a PLC at Work™, Leader's Guide is the best book for helping educators address both of these challenges in the area of English language arts. Douglas Fisher, Nancy Frey, and Cynthia L. Uline share their deep knowledge about the content standards in clear language that will resonate with practitioners. But they also recognize that the greater challenge facing educators is engaging in the structural and cultural changes that will allow the CCSS to flourish.

The authors understand that the most vital resource in the effort to raise student achievement through the Common Core State Standards for English language arts is not the content of the standards but the collective capacity of the educators in each school and district to engage in substantive school change that leads to more powerful teaching in more classrooms more of the time. They recognize that building this collective capacity requires high-quality professional development that is ongoing rather than sporadic. They understand that effective adult learning occurs in the workplace as educators engage in processes of continuous improvement rather than in occasional workshops. They know that the best professional development is embedded in the routine practices of the school and is collective and team based rather than individualistic. Perhaps most important, they stress that Common Core initiatives must focus directly and relentlessly on student achievement rather than adult activities.

This book provides much more than an overview of the Common Core State Standards for English language arts. It articulates the specific steps a school must take to move from a culture focused on covering English language arts curriculum to a culture fixated on each student's learning, from a culture of teacher isolation to a culture of purposeful collaboration and collective responsibility, from a culture where assessment is used as a tool to prove what students have learned to a culture where assessment is used to *improve* student learning, and from a culture where evidence of student learning is used primarily to assign grades to a culture where evidence of student learning is used to inform and improve professional practice.

In short, this book is exactly what district, school, and teacher leaders need as they face the challenge of implementing the CCSS. It merges the potential of the Common Core to serve as a positive force for student learning with the power of the Professional Learning Communities at Work™ (PLCs) process to provide a proven framework for school improvement. The authors draw on their expertise in English language arts content, good instruction, and the complexity of school change to present the comprehensive support educators will need as they face the challenge of bringing the Common Core to life in their schools and classrooms.

If you are interested in using the Common Core as a catalyst for improving both student and adult learning in English language arts, you won't find a better resource.

—Richard DuFour

INTRODUCTION

The investment of time and expertise by schools and districts to make the transformation into an effective Professional Learning Community at Work™ is about to pay off once again. The adoption of the Common Core State Standards for English language arts (CCSS ELA) represents a significant change in how the education profession looks at curriculum, instruction, and assessment. In addition, the implications for implementation of the CCSS ELA will have ramifications for years to come. As new research on best practices related to the Common Core State Standards is conducted and disseminated, educators will need to interpret these results and determine how best to put them into practice. The PLC process offers an ideal foundational system for doing so. This process provides the necessary conditions and support to accomplish the work of ensuring continuous improvement. Ongoing professional development is embedded into the process, because teachers work as members of high-performing collaborative teams. Becoming a PLC is a process of reculturing a school; the concept is not just another meeting (DuFour, DuFour, & Eaker, 2008; Frey, Fisher, & Everlove, 2009). Effective districtwide or schoolwide PLCs have the following six characteristics (DuFour et al., 2008; DuFour, DuFour, Eaker, & Many, 2010).

1. **Shared mission, vision, values, and goals all focused on student learning:** The *mission* defines why the organization exists; the *vision* defines what the organization can become in the future; the *values* consist of demonstrated attitudes and behaviors that further the vision; and the *goals* are markers used to determine results and assess progress. A thriving PLC immerses itself in the behaviors necessary to the development of these concepts.

2. **A collaborative culture with a focus on learning:** *Collaboration*, an essential ingredient in the PLC process, enables people to work interdependently to improve teaching and learning.

3. **Collective inquiry into best practice and current reality:** *Collective inquiry* is the process through which PLC educators strive to build shared knowledge about research and what works in their classrooms.

4. **Action orientation:** An *action orientation* is characteristic of successful PLCs that learn by doing and recognize the significance and necessity of actions that engage their members in planning learning tasks, implementing them, and evaluating results.

5. **A commitment to continuous improvement:** *Continuous improvement* is a cyclical process that PLCs use to plan, implement, and check to determine the effectiveness of their efforts to improve teaching and learning.

6. **Results orientation:** *Results* are what count for PLCs; they are the measurable outcomes that reveal the success of the collaborative efforts to improve teaching and learning. Results outweigh intentions.

Visit **www.allthingsplc.info** for a glossary of PLC terms.

These six characteristics must be woven into the fabric of the school; they have to become part of the air that teachers, parents, students, and administrators breathe. In creating this culture, PLCs must reach agreement on fundamental issues, including (DuFour et al., 2008):

- What content students should learn

- What common and coherent assessments to develop and use in order to determine if students have learned the agreed-on curriculum

- How to respond when students do or don't learn the agreed-on curriculum

To accomplish these three tasks, teachers need adequate time to collaborate with their colleagues. We are not suggesting that scheduling time for teachers to collaborate is easy, but without dedicated time, teams will not develop the collaborative structures needed to support student learning, especially if teachers are going to address the Common Core State Standards in their literacy programs. As part of their collaborative team time, teachers in PLCs engage in inquiry into student learning. The following four critical questions of a PLC highlight and provide a foundation for the work of collaborative planning teams (DuFour et al., 2008).

1. What do we want our students to learn?

2. How will we know when they have learned it?

3. How will we respond when some students don't learn?

4. How will we extend and enrich the learning for students who are already proficient?

Professional Development and Professional Learning Communities

Linda Darling-Hammond (2010) summarizes the research on effective professional development as follows:

> Effective professional development is sustained, ongoing, content-focused, and embedded in professional learning communities where teachers work overtime on problems of practice with other teachers in their subject area or school. Furthermore, it focuses on concrete tasks of teaching, assessment, observation, and reflection, looking at how students learn specific content in particular contexts. . . . It is often useful for teachers to be put in the position of studying the very material that they intend to teach to their own students. (pp. 226–227)

In other words, effective professional development is often the opposite of what most teachers receive—it is sustained and embedded within the work of professional learning communities and is focused on the actual tasks of teaching using the material teachers use with students. Professional development practices have moved beyond stand-alone workshops to ones that are tied to a school's chosen area of focus. Through the work of researchers like Bruce Joyce and Beverly Showers (1983) and others, educators began to understand that professional development could be linked to the change process. In particular, the value of an agreed-on focus, the need for continued support after the session, and a plan for measuring success have become expected elements of any school's professional development plan. To succeed as a high-performance school, professional development should be part of a teacher's overall involvement in a learning community.

The link between professional development and school change has been further strengthened through PLCs (Eaker, DuFour, & DuFour, 2002). PLCs recognize that teacher collaboration lies at the heart of learning and change. Collaborative planning teams within PLCs are able to bridge theory to practice as they convene regularly to examine student performance data, discuss student progress, develop and implement curricula, and coach one another through meaningful collaborative work between meetings.

The evidence of PLC effectiveness is mounting. A study of elementary teachers in PLCs identifies a strong statistical correlation between their participation in professional learning communities, their classroom cultures, and their use of formative assessments to advance learning (Birenbaum, Kimron, & Shilton, 2011). Robert Bullough and Steven Baugh (2008) find that the conditions created to foster a schoolwide PLC in turn deepened a school-university partnership. In an analysis of nearly four hundred schools as PLCs, Louise Stoll, Ray Bolam, Agnes McMahon, Mike Wallace, and Sally Thomas (2006) note a positive relationship between student achievement, adoption of innovative practices, and healthy learning communities. In fact, Robert Marzano notes that school and district-level PLCs are "probably the most influential movement with regards to actually changing practices in schools" (DuFour & Marzano, 2011, p. x).

Purpose of This Book

We hope we have made the case, however briefly, that a PLC at the school or district level is vital to school change. Furthermore, collaborative planning teams functioning within the school's PLC provide embedded professional development that sustains change.

In fact, chances are good that you are interested in this book because it promises to link an important change—implementing the Common Core State Standards for English language arts—with a process you already know to be powerful: professional learning communities. The remainder of this book provides leaders—principals, curriculum specialists, central office administrators, instructional coaches, department chairs, and teacher leaders—with information about the *what* and the *how* of teaching students to master these standards, including how to develop effective formative assessments and respond when students fail to make progress. We expand the Common Core State Standards so that you and your teams can examine them in detail. You will find that each chapter begins with questions for your teams to consider, and we invite you to return to these after you examine the standards to discuss implications for instruction, curriculum, assessment, and intervention.

Organization of This Book

This book has been crafted with your collaborative teams in mind. Use it as a workbook—mark it up, dog-ear the pages, highlight passages that resonate, and underline the ones that raise a question. In the same way that the Common Core ELA standards focus our collective attention on the practices of close reading and argumentation, we hope to contribute a similar process for your team in this book. The conversation begins in chapter 1 with a discussion about the role of leadership and inquiry in enacting the Common Core State Standards. Later in chapter 1, we focus on defining the vision and setting the direction for the implementation of the Common Core State Standards. In chapter 2, we explain how the standards are organized, so that the thirty-three-page original CCSS document and its three appendices become a bit less bewildering. It's also important to note what the standards don't say: about English learners (ELs), students with special needs, and those who struggle with literacy. The National Governors Association Center for Best Practices (NGA) and Council of Chief State School Officers (CCSSO), developers of the CCSS, provide some general guidelines for students learning English and those who struggle in school, but these are brief summaries and will likely generate a great number of additional ideas for implementation over the next several years (for more information, visit **go.solution-tree.com/commoncore** for links to the documents "Application of Common Core State Standards for English Language Learners" and "Application to Students With Disabilities," and visit www.ccsso.org/Resources /Resources_Listing.html for the document "Framework for English Language Proficiency Development Standards Corresponding to the Common Core State Standards and the

Next Generation Science Standards"). These gaps highlight why PLCs are so important. In the words of the NGA and CCSSO (2010a):

> While the Standards focus on what is most essential, they do not describe all that can or should be taught. A great deal is left to the discretion of teachers and curriculum developers. The aim of the Standards is to articulate the fundamentals, not to set out an exhaustive list or a set of restrictions that limits what can be taught beyond what is specified herein. (p. 6)

Chapter 3 focuses on the types of instruction that are necessary for teachers to actually implement the Common Core State Standards. In this chapter, we focus on high-quality core instruction and the types of experiences that students should have if they are to learn at high levels. Of course, what really matters is that students really do learn the content and that they are able to demonstrate their learning in a variety of formats. Chapter 4 focuses on the use of data to make instructional decisions. We discuss both hard and soft data that are required to determine if students really are learning. Chapter 4 also includes a discussion on using formative assessment processes and summative assessment instruments informatively and designing and implementing interventions for students who are not performing at expected levels. Finally, in chapter 5, we focus on the structures necessary to support teachers and students as they teach and learn at high levels.

Know that this book has been designed with you in mind. The research we cite is specific to grades K–12 language arts instruction. In addition, we've designed school-centered scenarios to illuminate the standards. The perspectives of school leaders, teachers, and students provide insight into ways collaborative teams engage to promote effective teaching and learning. The scenarios are fictionalized accounts of our personal teaching activities and our collective experience working with teachers across grade levels in schools with diverse populations. We present these scenarios as a way to make the ELA standards come alive for you. We want you to personalize this experience as you and your collaborative teams plan for implementation of the Common Core for English language arts. To begin this process, we encourage you to reflect on and discuss with your colleagues the following questions.

1. What is the status of collaborative teams at your school? Acknowledging the reality of your school's commitment to an effective PLC process is a critical first step that can establish the future direction for collaborative professional growth. Recall the six characteristics of effective PLCs (pages 1–2), and consider the extent to which your PLC embodies these characteristics. If you want to delve deeper into your school's PLC status, you can explore where your school would place on the PLC continuum: preinitiating, initiating, implementing, developing, or sustaining (DuFour, DuFour, Eaker, & Many, 2010). Visit www.allthingsplc.info and search the Tools & Resources section for helpful PLC reproducibles, such as the PLC continuum reproducible "Laying the Foundation" from *Learning by Doing* (DuFour, DuFour, Eaker, & Many, 2010).

2. How are your students performing? Are there areas of need in terms of curriculum development? Are there areas of need in terms of instruction? Are there areas of need in terms of assessment? These questions address key topics for your PLC to consider as you focus on the current status of your school's language arts programs in relation to the expectations of the Common Core ELA standards. Discussions with your collaborative teams will enable you to gain insight into *where you are* and *where you need to go* to support and advance your students' language development.

We've designed this book to guide the conversations that are necessary to fully implement the Common Core State Standards. As such, it should serve as a resource that you return to regularly to consider the ways in which student learning can be improved. The anchor standards and the grade-level expectations are the outcomes expected of students, and teachers and leaders are in the position of guiding student learning through collaborative efforts. *Common Core English Language Arts in a PLC at Work™, Leader's Guide* provides the process to get there.

CHAPTER 1

Leading Schoolwide Inquiry Around the Common Core State Standards

KEY QUESTIONS

- What actions in your previous leadership experience have fostered development of effective collaborative planning teams? How will you use that experience to lead schoolwide inquiry around the CCSS?

- What is your vision for implementing the CCSS ELA with teachers in your school? What first steps do you plan for developing and communicating the vision?

- What aspects of the school culture will contribute to success in implementing the CCSS ELA? What aspects of that culture do you think will be obstacles to success?

- What do you think is the biggest challenge you face in leading schoolwide inquiry around the CCSS ELA?

Teachers at an elementary school are accustomed to meeting regularly as a faculty. Their former principal led them in reviewing and discussing student data and directed grade-level teams to develop common assessments as a means of monitoring student progress. Three consecutive years of lackluster results left teachers and the school district disappointed with the absence of return on the time and energy invested. According to fifth-grade teacher Theresa Hughes, "I am frustrated by the fact that I was collaborating and planning with colleagues, monitoring student progress, and developing interventions for students who struggled, but we observed no notable progress." She then qualifies her statement, "To be honest, I can remember when our meetings included the principal's announcements and directives. Too often, we were left with little time for collaboration or professional development, and so we struggled to understand our data. We were probably shooting in the dark when it came to our instructional responses and interventions. In fact, we never really had the time to unpack our state standards together and develop curriculum in an informed way. It's difficult to admit, but our cursory understanding of the standards probably resulted in mediocre first teaching. We were always running to catch up and relying on after-the-fact intervention to fill in the gaps."

Recently, the elementary school hired a new principal, and teachers recognize that this principal appreciates the significance of time. Principal Linda Diaz understands the necessary prerequisites to genuine collaboration and plans accordingly. She acknowledges,

"Teachers need to grasp the standards and design corresponding assessments. They need time to investigate the data, interpret it, and decide what to do about it. And, they need to do this together."

Principal Diaz agrees to forego operational meetings, covering these items through email or memo. She recoups this regularly scheduled meeting time, works with teachers to eliminate waste and capture additional minutes within the daily schedule, and extends the time even further through grant dollars that would pay for substitute teachers. The resultant time allows for regularly scheduled meetings during which collaborative grade-level planning teams engage in ongoing, job-embedded professional development. Teachers spend half of their sessions establishing learning goals, monitoring student progress toward these established goals, analyzing formative assessment data, refining assessments where necessary, and sharing strategies for intervention and support. The second half of the sessions consists of grade-level planning, now around learning the Common Core State Standards using a four-part protocol for inquiry: (1) What is familiar? (2) What is new? (3) What may be challenging for students? (4) What may be challenging for teachers? As teachers take time to understand and master the learning standards; study the current trends in student performance; investigate the causes of students' academic weaknesses; and adjust curriculum, instruction, assessment, and intervention accordingly, new norms of openness and collective responsibility emerge.

The provision of regular and sustained time for job-embedded inquiry and professional development constitutes a bold and courageous move on the part of Principal Diaz. Some school leaders view this gift of time as an unnecessary expense. Others consider it an impossible dream. Principal Diaz maintains that time is an important step to building a culture of active inquiry and learning for all stakeholders. According to fourth-grade teacher Ross Jeffries, "Our new principal knows how to nurture authentic collaboration. First, she focuses our efforts, and then she provides the time needed for professional dialogue and learning."

Time Is the Essence

Even before we examine the leadership behaviors and practices that will assist you as a leader in implementing the CCSS ELA, we underscore the importance of carefully structured and focused time as fundamental to teacher collaboration and professional development. Without dedicated time, you and your teachers will be unable to develop the collaborative structures needed to support student learning, especially learning according to the CCSS ELA. Unlike most state standards from the 1990s, the Common Core State Standards require an integrated approach to lesson development through which teachers build students' competence across multiple standards simultaneously. This now essential practice of integrated instruction, coupled with significant shifts in thinking about literacy development as evolving readiness for college and careers, may require fundamental changes to curricular content and teaching practice at your school. These new habits of practice are nuanced and, by necessity, interrelated, thus requiring time to develop and refine.

We know that scheduling time for teachers to collaborate is never easy. However, time is a precious commodity that you need to secure, protect, and leverage for teachers to have the opportunity to work together in collaborative teams. In doing so, they can ensure learning for *all* students. It is imperative that collaborative team members work to answer the four critical questions of a PLC as they devote attention to the CCSS (DuFour et al., 2008).

1. What do we want our students to learn?

2. How will we know when they have learned it?

3. How will we respond when some students don't learn?

4. How will we extend and enrich the learning for students who are already proficient?

Findings from a number of studies emphasize the vital roles school leaders play in providing and protecting sufficient time for teachers to meet as collaborative planning teams, guiding the vision and subsequent professional development goals that will be pursued during this time and providing necessary resources to support the ongoing inquiry that is central to the work of these teams (Louis, Marks, & Kruse, 1996; Mullen & Hutinger, 2008; Olivier & Hipp, 2006). Such support is especially critical as teachers unpack the CCSS. Notably, teachers need to plan together, look at student work together, identify needs for reteaching together, trust one another, and ask for help when they need it.

Inquiry Is the Engine

Principals and teachers are expected to apply the habits and skills of keen diagnosis, scrupulous implementation, and rigorous evaluation as a matter of course. National, state, and local accountability systems challenge school leaders to collect, record, interpret, and present objective evidence that shows all students are achieving desired outcomes. To be responsible within this highly charged policy context and, at the same time, responsive to the needs of increasingly diverse school communities, school leaders must provide data-informed instructional guidance, empower teachers to make sound instructional decisions, and develop and implement strategic school improvement plans (Leithwood, Louis, Anderson, & Wahlstrom, 2004).

As the web of school, community, and governance (from accountability plans, school boards, and district pressure) grows increasingly more complex, school leaders must master clear and elegant ways to think about their work. Additionally, they must lead others to do the same, constructing knowledge about their school through engagement in active and artful inquiry and problem solving (Creasap, Peters, & Uline, 2005; Perez & Uline, 2003; Uline, 1997). While by no means a new construct, inquiry is increasingly considered a primary *engine of reform*, providing a means to change and sustain school practices and culture "in ways that enhance the quality and equity of teaching and learning" (Center for Research on the Context of Teaching, 2002, p. 23). As principals and teachers learn together to focus and systematize inquiry, their "professional community becomes more collaborative and mutually accountable and leadership becomes more distributed, proactive, and sustainable" (p. 23). Through inquiry, you and your teachers make connections across learning problems and leverage various solutions and sources of support. Teachers discover that they are not the only ones struggling to help particular students master particular standards. What works in someone else's classroom just might work in theirs.

Furthermore, inquiry offers you a tool to cultivate the growth of organizational expertise as you and your teachers, repeatedly and over extended periods of time, interact to resolve any school improvement challenge. With expertise grows a collective sense of confidence in the organization's ability to meet various challenges, such as the adoption of the Common Core State Standards. As we discuss in the next section, in the hands of effective leaders, PLC-based inquiry becomes a means to *define the vision and set the direction, develop teachers and build their capacity, redesign school structures and systems,* and *improve the instructional program* in ways that will support successful implementation of the CCSS (Leithwood & Riehl, 2005).

Your Leadership Is Significant

A growing body of evidence underscores a significant and positive relationship between effective principal leadership and student learning and achievement. Research includes qualitative case studies of highly challenged, high-performing schools (Johnson, 2002; Johnson & Asera, 1999; Johnson, Lein, & Ragland, 1998; Maden, 2001; Scheurich, 1998) and quantitative studies examining indirect leadership effects on student outcomes (Alig-Mielcarek & Hoy, 2005; Hallinger, Bickman, & Davis, 1996; Heck, 1992, 2000; Heck, Larsen, & Marcoulides, 1990; Leithwood & Jantzi, 1999; Marks & Printy, 2003; Robinson, Lloyd, & Rowe, 2008). In fact, an extensive review of evidence related to the nature and size of these effects concludes that among school-related factors, leadership is second only to classroom instruction in its contribution to student learning (Leithwood et al., 2004). Furthermore, these effects are greatest within contexts where they are most needed; that is, "The greater the challenge the greater the impact of [leader] actions on learning" (Leithwood et al., 2004, p. 3).

Across the research, effective leadership actions are organized in similar fashion, observing that successful leaders rely on a set of core practices, which when applied in combination result in improved learning results for students. These four core domains of practice are the following (Hallinger & Heck, 1999; Leithwood, 2005; Leithwood et al., 2004; Leithwood & Riehl, 2005; Leithwood & Sun, 2012; Waters, Marzano, & McNulty, 2003).

1. Define and advance organizational purpose, vision, and direction.

2. Develop people and encourage their individual and collective sense of efficacy for the work.

3. Redesign and improve organizational structures, systems, and contexts.

4. Manage and improve the instructional program.

Together, these four core domains of practice provide a useful organizing framework for inquiry and action as principals lead teachers to implement the Common Core State Standards. For successful implementation, school leaders should:

- Define the vision and set the direction to implement the CCSS

- Develop teachers and build their capacity to teach the CCSS

- Redesign school structures and systems to support CCSS implementation

- Manage and improve the instructional program to embrace the CCSS

Define the Vision and Set the Direction to Implement the CCSS

A middle school's retreat takes place in late summer at a nearby regional park's free conference space. Prior to the retreat, Principal Jake Monroe spends time developing an initial vision of the school's eighth-grade graduates leaving middle school with a strong grasp of the CCSS for grades 6–8 and fully prepared to meet the rigors of the high school standards. He invites a team of teacher leaders, including especially strong teachers from each of the core content areas and the school's math and English language arts instructional coaches, to assist him in honing this vision. Together, the teacher leader team and Principal Monroe put the vision before the other teachers for comment and further refinement. Principal Monroe sees the retreat as a means to signal a new direction. He knows that the Common Core State Standards will test teachers' resolve in continuing the hard work of instructional improvement. He knows he needs to motivate and inspire, demonstrating in no uncertain terms that this current challenge is attainable. He knows he needs to provide tangible evidence that the teachers are well positioned to take this next step.

During the first hour of the retreat, Principal Monroe and the lead teacher team present the vision and take teachers' suggestions for refinement. The remainder of the day is spent developing an action plan for student success in learning the Common Core State Standards.

Principal Monroe says, "Across the eight-hour day, we apply some carefully choreographed facilitation. Our collective inquiry is focused on the necessary action steps we will follow to understand and implement these new learning standards in a way that builds on our current momentum. We aren't going to digest these new standards in a day, but we can develop a powerful vision of how our program will look once we have. And, we can set a direction for how we will get there. People leave the retreat feeling way less intimidated and way more confident that we can do this. It is time well spent!"

Effective leaders take time to develop a shared vision of the future. They do this in consort with their teachers, engaging their minds and their energies in plotting a path of achievable goals and action steps for accomplishing them (Leithwood, 2005; Leithwood et al., 2004; Leithwood & Riehl, 2005). As you begin to consider what teachers specifically need to know to implement the CCSS ELA with fidelity, you are wise to also step back and contemplate how you will craft a powerful vision of students who are mastering these standards in ways that prepare them for college and careers. This vision will motivate teachers and channel their individual and collective energies. The corresponding goals you and your teachers develop should be personally compelling, and so, in the case of the CCSS, your teachers must be convinced that these standards will help them do their jobs more effectively and efficiently. If you structure short-term goals in a way that challenges teachers without overwhelming them, you will help teachers make sense of their work. Then, as you continue to monitor organizational performance around the goals and communicate the results broadly, you'll continue to bolster a strong sense of shared organizational purpose.

Of course, effective principals don't stop here. They continue to build the individual and organizational capacity to enact the vision. They empower teachers to take risks and flex their own leadership potential, offering each other the necessary provocations and supports to push their collective inquiry forward. Teachers face a sense of cognitive dissonance brought on by state and federal policies that reveal inequities in students' opportunities to learn and achieve. Implementation of the Common Core State Standards may only exacerbate this sense of discomfort and frustration, as more challenging learning standards and expectations may reveal even wider gaps in students' learning. Effective principals will seek to develop their teachers and build their capacity to acquire "new sets of knowledge, skills, ways of thinking, and . . . values" (Waters et al., 2003, p. 51) and challenge myths about who is or is not capable of mastering these more challenging learning standards.

Develop Teachers and Build Their Capacity to Teach the CCSS

The action steps set forth in a high school's plan for implementing the Common Core State Standards include increased opportunities for teachers to observe each other teaching the standards. Principal Donna Caldwell works with teachers and the counseling staff to adjust the master schedule in a way that incorporates rotating opportunities for teachers to observe demonstration lessons (Principal Caldwell teaches some lessons in her content area, English) and participate in cross-classroom visitations. Under Principal Caldwell's direction, grade-level collaborative planning teams also establish peer-coaching partnerships. Felicia Brownswell, a tenth-grade biology teacher, describes the experience of working with her partner, "The beauty of working together on learning and implementing these standards is that when we come together and plan, there's this wonderful third woman who emerges, and she's smarter than both of us! We are figuring it out together and taking our growing knowledge back to our department's collaborative planning team. Everyone benefits, especially our students."

The high school teachers grow more adept in their understanding and teaching of the CCSS, because their peers and principal coach and model these skills. Principal Caldwell uses her role as instructional leader to develop the instructional leadership capacity of her teachers.

Traditional notions of instructional leadership emphasize the principal's coordination and control of classroom instruction in heroic fashion, developing teachers' capacity through top-down supervision and evaluation (Cohen & Miller, 1980; Heck et al., 1990). Research critiques these more conventional notions, emphasizing the limitations of middle-manager authority to provide direct supervision of teaching, as well as the inappropriateness of what some perceive as a hierarchical approach that fails to acknowledge teachers as the school's primary instructional experts (Hallinger, 2003; Marks & Printy, 2003).

More effectively, instructional leadership should be "conceptualized as a *mutual influence process*, rather than as a one-way process in which leaders influence others" (Hallinger, 2003, p. 346). Such a view underscores the role of instructional leadership, at the same time acknowledging "its evolving nature in the context of teacher professionalism" (Marks & Printy, 2003, p. 391). Research during and since the 1990s advances more reciprocal and inclusive models of instructional leadership within which principals share their authority with instructional coaches and classroom teachers (Heck, 1992; Heck et al., 1990; Mangin, 2007; Marks & Printy, 2003). Here, empowering principals encourage collaborative inquiry rather than rely on more conventional, principal-centered supervisory practices (Blase & Blase, 1999; Halverson, Grigg, Prichett, & Thomas, 2007; Murphy, Elliot, Goldring, & Porter, 2007; Reitzug, 1997). In response to these shared instructional leadership practices, teachers grow in their commitment, involvement, and willingness to innovate (Sheppard, 1996; Supovitz & Riggan, 2012; Supovitz, Sirinides, & May, 2010).

In a mixed-methods investigation of twenty-four selected elementary, middle, and high schools, eight at each school level, Marks and Printy (2003) discover seven schools that outperformed the others in quality of pedagogy and student achievement. They note that in these schools the principal combined transformational leadership and shared instructional leadership with teachers. As transformational leaders, these principals serve as role models, coaching or mentoring their teachers, motivating and inspiring them, and building teachers' confidence in their ability to accomplish goals (Bass, 1985; Leithwood, 2005). The principals at these seven schools are strong instructional leaders but at the same time, "they facilitated leadership by the teachers, whom they regarded as professionals and full partners in furthering high quality teaching and learning" (Marks & Printy, 2003, p. 387). When principals combine transformational leadership behaviors with shared instructional leadership strategies, schools show significant progress in their reform efforts and increase student achievement.

As you seek to develop your teachers' capacity for teaching the Common Core State Standards, it will be important for you to provide multiple, ongoing opportunities for reflective dialogue, open sharing of classroom practices, the development of common knowledge about the standards, and collaboration on developing new materials and curricula. In order for teachers to successfully adapt and refine their teaching practices to meet the changing expectations of the CCSS, they must have opportunities within their collaborative planning teams to participate in what Ralph Putnam and Hilda Borko (1997) call *classroom discourse communities*:

> Just as students cannot learn science by interacting with the physical world without interaction with others who know science, teachers are unlikely to transcend their current view of teaching practice without an influx of ideas or ways of thinking about teaching, learning, and subject matter from another source. Just as students need to learn new ways of reasoning, communicating, and thinking, and to acquire dispositions of inquiry and sense-making through their participation in classroom discourse communities, teachers need to construct their complex new roles and ways of thinking about their teaching practice within the context of supportive learning communities. (pp. 1247, 1250)

These collaborative planning teams provide opportunities for teachers to reflect deeply and critically on their own teaching practices, the content they teach, and the experiences and backgrounds of the learners in their classrooms. Sharing with one another in this way supports the risk taking and struggle entailed in transforming practice. It can also help teachers impose meaning and organization on incoming information in light of their existing knowledge and beliefs (Putnam & Borko, 1997).

No doubt, your teachers will call on their current knowledge as they grapple with the Common Core State Standards' conceptual shifts in understanding how students develop content knowledge. (For details regarding these shifts, see chapter 2, pages 20–24.) They will draw on their current knowledge as they stretch to meet the expectations of the anchor standards. (For details about anchor standards, see chapter 2, pages 27–37.) The anchor standards require that students begin from the primary grades forward to develop their capabilities in six ways: (1) as independent learners with mastery of strong content knowledge; (2) as communicators who respond to the varying demands of audience, task, purpose, and discipline; (3) as thinkers who can comprehend as well as critique; (4) as inquirers who value evidence; (5) as digital natives who use technology and digital media strategically; and (6) as culturally competent global citizens. These new understandings and expectations will require that teachers look across instructional units, the school year, content areas, and grade and school levels to build a purposeful plan for scaffolding students' capacity for this complex and interrelated set of knowledge and skills. Such a comprehensive view of curricular and instructional practice may push you to consider new structures and systems to facilitate the work.

Redesign School Structures and Systems to Support CCSS Implementation

To direct the ongoing work of grade-level collaborative planning teams, Principal Monroe calls on the same group of teacher leaders who had assisted in refining the school's vision of successful CCSS implementation, which includes content-area teachers and instructional coaches. Principal Monroe summons this group to assist him in maintaining the focus of collaborative planning team meetings, ensuring continuity from meeting to meeting, and comparing the work across grade levels and content areas. To accomplish this, each teacher leader meets regularly with an assigned collaborative planning team to monitor and support its work. Principal Monroe meets monthly with the core leadership team to receive feedback, check progress, adjust strategy, and disseminate necessary curricular and instructional information across the faculty. Principal Monroe redefines faculty responsibilities, balancing the focus of teachers' ongoing inquiry across individual student, classroom, and schoolwide progress. These new activities and arrangements encourage teachers to view their work from a new vantage point.

The Common Core State Standards will require this integrated, multilevel approach. Excellent teaching within individual classrooms will not suffice. Your teachers must contribute to the corporate mission. They must be planners, organizers, researchers, instigators, and experimenters. In this regard, the school must move even further along the continuum from local practices to universal and public practices. Not all of the teachers at Principal Monroe's school have an ideal balance of schoolwide, team, and individual emphasis, and yet this is Principal Monroe's goal.

Asking teachers to shift their fundamental beliefs and practices presents a formidable challenge. For some schools, implementation of the CCSS will involve refinement and extension of work already under way. For other schools, implementing new standards may necessitate a transformation in curricular and instructional norms of practice. Either way, the challenges that you and your teachers will face will be made all the more substantial as you attempt to initiate change while in the midst of conducting your everyday business. Engaging in significant change involves a period of disequilibrium that can leave teachers and administrators anxious, uncertain, and stressed (Uline, Tschannen-Moran, & Perez, 2003), even if the changes also bring renewed excitement and vigor.

In the face of new challenges, effective leaders quell fears and maintain productive learning cultures by adjusting structures and systems that no longer adequately support the work of teachers and students (Leithwood et al., 2004). As you face these changing expectations, you may find it necessary to modify structures and build new collaborative processes in order to better realize effective and efficient progress toward shared goals. In the case of the Common Core, the fundamental goal remains constant: *improve instructional effectiveness to ensure all students are college and career ready in English language arts*. Still, the nuances of these new learning standards require increased levels of curricular and instructional integration. As school leaders investigate possible structures and systems to support the implementation of the CCSS, they are wise to direct their inquiry toward "both the classroom conditions that students experience directly and the wider organizational conditions that enable, stimulate, and support these conditions" (Leithwood & Sun, 2012, p. 413). For example, as you initiate teachers' examination of the CCSS ELA related to text complexity (see chapter 2, page 21), collaborative teams can focus discussion on how these particular standards will influence choices related to curricular materials and instructional approaches. Furthermore, you might also explore how this work can take place across two collaborative planning team configurations, as teachers work within grade levels as well as across grades to articulate a cohesive plan. These horizontal and vertical team collaborations will help ensure that students experience a cohesive curriculum without gaps or redundancy.

The simultaneous focus on the technical core of learning and teaching along with the organizational purposes, structures, and processes that influence it will help you, as principal, leverage the focus and energy of your school's collaborative teams to accomplish the necessary changes in instructional and curricular norms of practice.

Manage and Improve the Instructional Program to Embrace the CCSS

When it comes to improving the instructional program at Principal Diaz's elementary school, she emphasizes that time *is* the essence (see page 8). She persistently and strategically eases her way into classrooms, offering feedback and modeling lessons in a way that demonstrates her respect for teachers and her own love of teaching. According to Principal Diaz, her efforts to improve the instructional program start with winning teachers' trust. Rebecca Straus, a fourth-grade teacher, acknowledges these efforts: "From the outset, Principal Diaz expresses her intention to be in classrooms between 8:30 and 11:30 each morning. She tells parents, staff, and district office personnel that only genuine emergencies will pull her away from this routine. It took us awhile to be comfortable with this, and some teachers are still wary, but I for one begin to miss her input if too many days go by when I don't look up and see her sitting next to one of my students."

As the elementary school moves toward full implementation of the Common Core State Standards, Principal Diaz tells teachers that she will be looking for student engagement focused on clearly articulated instructional objectives. Teachers know that when she comes to observe, she will quietly ask individual students to describe what they are learning and why the objective is important. According to Principal Diaz, "Engagement means they are following the objective. They're on task. I ask the students three questions: 'What are you learning? Why are you learning it? How will you know you have mastered it?'"

Principal Diaz knows the CCSS will require that she pay particular attention to the level of rigor, or cognitive complexity, demanded of students as they pursue the lesson objective. She explains, "I want to see students thinking, grappling, writing, and articulating their thoughts. If all students are able to answer all of the questions, something is wrong—they're not learning new information."

While Principal Diaz expects to see a high level of challenge and difficulty in student work, she also looks for strong evidence that students understand the concepts and skills being taught. She expects to see students reviewing each other's work, summarizing, using rubrics or scoring guides, making connections to real events or issues, probing, questioning, writing, explaining, verifying, and relating.

Principal Diaz's efforts to improve the elementary school's instructional program are collaborative, but they are also hands-on. Her presence and active inquiry within classrooms, coupled with her participation in the ongoing inquiry of grade-level collaborative planning team meetings, keep her abreast of schoolwide progress toward CCSS ELA implementation. She is genuinely excited to tell teachers when she learns something new from observing their teaching, and she does so often. Through her observation of individual teachers' struggles and triumphs, as well as her probing of students' understanding of learning objectives, Principal Diaz learns firsthand how far teachers have progressed in changing the school's curricular and instructional norms. She is also able to notice when teachers need support, guidance, and materials. Her timely provision of assistance further nurtures trust between her and her teachers.

As leaders of a school's instructional program, principals are encouraged to spend considerable time in classrooms observing teaching and learning (DiPaola & Hoy, 2008; Downey, Steffy, English, Frase, & Poston, 2004; Glickman, Gordon, & Ross-Gordon, 2004; Ing, 2009). Frequent classroom observations allow school leaders time to notice firsthand what is going on in classrooms, which better positions them to monitor instruction, provide appropriate resources and supports to teachers, and influence the instructional climate of their schools (Ing, 2009; Johnson, Uline, & Perez, 2011). Furthermore, classroom observations are "the way they see and understand these classrooms and . . . the way they make judgments about whether they see instances of good or bad teaching, [which provides principals opportunities to] . . . affect teachers' efforts to change their instructional practice" (Nelson & Sassi, 2000, p. 554).

The implementation of the Common Core State Standards provides school leaders new leverage in their continuing efforts to improve instructional effectiveness at their schools. The standards will require students to stretch for higher, more complex levels of subject-matter thinking. They will require heightened levels of integration across content areas and grade levels. They will draw attention to the knowledge and skills necessary for college and careers from the primary grades up. More so than ever, school leaders' classroom-level observations and inquiries will need to focus on "the central intellectual ideas of the lesson, . . . pay[ing] attention to how they are being developed within the classroom's structures and practices" (Nelson & Sassi, 2000, p. 574). Teachers will need this close examination of their practice from you and from their peers in order to discern if they are making the grade in challenging their students to high levels of engagement with the subject-area content.

In a study of effective instructional leadership from teachers' points of view, 809 teachers responded to an open-ended questionnaire through which they described specific principal characteristics that enhance classroom instruction (Blase & Blase, 1999). According to research participants, central among these characteristics are the abilities to *hold up a mirror* and serve as *another set of eyes*, providing detailed and specific feedback focused on observed classroom behavior within a problem-solving orientation based on trust and respect. Hold up the mirror for your teachers. Help them to gauge the level of engagement they are able to elicit from their students. Provide them with specific and detailed feedback on how and when students actively participate in the learning activities they design to teach challenging academic objectives. Share your observations of particular students' attempts to explain and describe key concepts, noting the degree to which this student talk demonstrates understanding of the lesson content.

Hold up a mirror to their classroom environments as well, and provide examples of how these environments are academically and intellectually stimulating, warm and welcoming, and orderly without being rigid.

Conclusion

Though collaborative inquiry is never simple or easy, it holds significant promise for schools that seek to implement the Common Core State Standards in a manner that will sustain, rather than derail, their ongoing school improvement efforts. Even as school leaders and teachers face the challenges of reinventing their work in response to the Common Core State Standards, their collaborative inquiry provides a powerful mechanism for becoming smarter about the technical core of their work. As teachers continue to collaborate with one another, they create a context within which existing knowledge and beliefs about teaching practice are challenged and, in some cases, transformed. As principals focus their own inquiry to define the vision and set the direction, develop teachers and build their capacity, redesign school structures and systems, and manage and improve the instructional program for implementing the CCSS, teachers and other school staff will benefit if principals' thinking is visible and their values and goals that guide their decisions are explicit. In this way, all who participate in this reform effort will keep the fundamental goal constant: *improve instructional effectiveness to ensure all students are college and career ready in English language arts.*

CHAPTER 2

Leading Your School Through the Common Core State Standards

KEY QUESTIONS

- To what extent do you and your teachers understand the conceptual shifts represented in the Common Core State Standards for English language arts?

- In which of the four strands—Reading, Writing, Speaking and Listening, or Language—do you think teachers will have to make the most significant adjustments in their practice? Why do you think that will be the case?

- What do you think will be the impact on school resources and planning as a result of implementing the Common Core ELA? Which areas will be most affected?

School leaders face an enormous task in leading schools through the change process, and without question, the major change will be implementing the CCSS. The adoption of these standards extends a trend in the education field to collaborate across organizations in order to obtain better learning results. Standards-driven policies and practices have yielded notable results, especially in our collective efforts to articulate purposes and learning outcomes to our stakeholders (Gamoran, 2007). This in turn has led to improved alignment among curriculum, instruction, and assessment. However, there are weaknesses in this system, including the disjointed efforts of individual states trying to put their own standards in motion. No matter how effective their process or product, states simply could not share them with other states, as no standards were held in common. Consequently, states like Arkansas and Arizona could not pool human and fiscal resources to develop common materials and assessments.

As standards-based assessments rose to prominence in the 2000s, a mosaic of testing results made it virtually impossible to fairly compare the effectiveness of reform efforts across states. The National Governors Association Center for Best Practices and the Council of Chief State School Officers sought to rectify these shortcomings by sponsoring the development of a shared set of standards each state could agree on. Beginning in 2010, state boards of education began adopting these standards in English language arts and mathematics. By 2012, nearly all the states had adopted them and begun to determine timelines for implementation, as well as methods for assessment.

In an effort to capitalize on new opportunities for collaboration among states, two assessment consortia are developing standards-based assessments. Both the Partnership for Assessment of Readiness for College and Careers (PARCC) and the Smarter Balanced Assessment Consortium (SBAC) consist of representatives from states working to develop assessments of the standards. Some states belong to both and will eventually determine which instruments they will use. While these efforts are works in progress, common themes emerge from both consortia. For one, it is likely that a significant part of the tests will be computer based. In addition, it is anticipated that benchmark assessments will play a prominent role in schools being better able to identify students who are falling behind. But perhaps the biggest shift in these assessments has to do with the ELA standards themselves. These standards and assessments call for significant shifts in what students will need to know and be able to do. Understanding the following five shifts is essential in order to lead the implementation process. (Visit www.parcconline.org or www.smarterbalanced.org for more information.)

Shift One: Focus on Reading and Writing to Inform, Persuade, and Convey Experiences

The Common Core ELA standards reflect a trend in literacy that has been occurring since the 1990s: a deepening appreciation of the importance of informational and persuasive texts in a student's *reading diet*, or the range of reading genre and materials students encounter across the school year. (For now, we will focus our discussion on informational texts, with further attention to persuasive texts featured later in this chapter in the section on argumentation.) The reasons for increasing informational text usage are often related to the need to improve content knowledge (Moss, 2005), to meet increased demand in digital environments (Schmar-Dobler, 2003), and even to prevent the so-called *fourth-grade slump* (Chall & Jacobs, 2003), which suggests that student achievement stagnates in fourth grade.

The National Assessment of Educational Progress (NAEP), sometimes called "the nation's report card," has steadily increased the use of informational text passages on its assessments of fourth-, eighth-, and twelfth-grade students across the United States. In keeping with this initiative, the CCSS ELA recommend an evenly divided diet of literary and informational texts in the elementary years, gradually increasing to more informational texts throughout middle and high school (see table 2.1).

Table 2.1: Grade Distribution of Literary and Informational Passages in the 2009 NAEP Framework

Grade	Literary Texts	Informational Texts
4	50 percent	50 percent
8	45 percent	55 percent
12	30 percent	70 percent

Source: Adapted from NGA & CCSSO, 2010a, p. 5.

Keep in mind that this doesn't mean that students in middle school and high school should no longer be allowed to read narrative text; nothing could be further from the truth. Narrative remains essential as a means of conveying ideas and concepts through story. However, just as a nutritional diet limited to only one or two foods cannot provide sufficient nourishment, neither should we limit the types of texts used in the classroom. Furthermore, it is helpful to consider use of informational texts across the school day, not only in the reading and language arts block or in English courses, in which teachers use a greater volume of literary texts. Collaborative planning teams that do not fully understand the call for more informational text usage across the day may mistakenly eliminate all literary texts to the detriment of student learning.

Shift Two: Focus on Increasing Text Complexity

Closely related to an emphasis on informational text is "steadily increasing text complexity" (NGA & CCSSO, 2010b, p. 2). This aspect has received considerable attention as educators figure out how to apply a three-part model for determining how complex a reading really is. In addition, U.S. school teams are working to design methods for accessing complex texts among students who struggle to read, for English learners, and for students with special needs. The CCSS ELA define text complexity as "the inherent difficulty of reading and comprehending a text combined with consideration of reader and task variables; in the Standards, a three-part assessment of text difficulty that pairs qualitative [factors] and quantitative measures with reader-task considerations" (NGA & CCSSO, 2010b, p. 43). In other words, it is multidimensional, with attention given to (1) *quantitative measures*, such as readability formulae; (2) *qualitative factors*, such as complexity of ideas, organization, and cohesion; and (3) *reader and task considerations*, such as motivation and task difficulty.

The issue of text complexity raises the case for backward planning, with the outcome being that graduating high school students are sufficiently prepared to tackle the kinds of texts they will encounter as they enter college and careers. Appendix B of the Common Core ELA (NGA & CCSSO, 2010c) includes an extensive list of text exemplars to illustrate this concept of text complexity. These text exemplars should not be misconstrued as a required reading list for a specific grade. To do so would ignore the third dimension of identifying complex texts: reader and task considerations.

Referenced within the standards is a *staircase* effect to systematically develop students' capacity for understanding more complex texts (NGA & CCSSO, 2010a). The staircase should be considered at several levels of analysis: within a unit of instruction, throughout a school year, and across multiple grades. That is, the texts a student uses at the beginning of a unit to build background knowledge are more explicit, while those that occur later in a unit to deepen student knowledge are less so. Similarly, the texts students utilize early in a given school year are less complex than those that occur near the end. Additionally, students' capacity and stamina for reading complex texts should build across grade-level bands. For this reason, work concerning text complexity should involve at least two collaborative planning team configurations—as teachers work within grades as well as across grade bands (K–2, 3–5, 6–8, and 9–12)—to articulate a cohesive plan. These horizontal and vertical team collaborations ensure that students experience a cohesive curriculum without gaps or redundancy.

Text complexity poses a major challenge for educators as students transition to classroom environments that increasingly rely on texts as a major source of learning. Defining what makes a text complex requires analyzing qualitative factors and quantitative measures, while also considering the characteristics of the reader and the demands of the related task. In addition, the CCSS encourage teachers to look across units, the school year, and grade bands to build a purposeful plan to staircase student capacity for complex texts.

Shift Three: Focus on Speaking and Listening

The CCSS place a strong emphasis on speaking and listening in the primary grades. Furthermore, NGA and CCSSO (2010b) state:

> The importance of oral language extends well beyond the earliest grades. . . . Sticht and James found evidence strongly suggesting that children's listening comprehension outpaces reading comprehension until the middle school years (grades 6–8). (p. 26)

Speaking and listening skills have a concomitant relationship with reading and writing development. To observe this effect, Virginia Berninger and Robert Abbott (2010) examine two cohorts of students from elementary and into middle school, measuring their listening comprehension, oral expression, reading comprehension, and writing comprehension in grades 1, 3, 5, and 7. They discover students' relative strengths and weaknesses vary considerably across the years, supporting the assertion that these language modalities are not fixed but rather are influenced considerably by experiences and education. The researchers note:

> Some [people] still believe that children learn oral language before they come to school and that the purpose of schooling is to teach written language. . . . When the four separate language systems are well integrated and synchronized, language may be experienced as a unitary construct, much as rain is experienced as unitary wetness rather than as isolated drops. (p. 649)

Berninger and Abbott (2010) advocate for a view of "comprehension and expression via language by ear, mouth, hand, and eye" (p. 635); however, collaborative planning teams may fail to examine these Speaking and Listening standards within the context of the Reading and Writing strands. School leaders should encourage teachers to build robust curricula that weave these experiences into as many instructional events as possible.

Shift Four: Focus on Text-Based Evidence for Argumentation

A fourth shift concerns the development of argumentation skills. This may be unfamiliar to many elementary teachers who typically have experience at rhetorical reading and writing only as college students themselves. Argumentation as a formal process isn't present in the Common Core ELA until grades 6–12. However, the foundation for it is built in the elementary years through opinion. Importantly, *opinion* doesn't refer to the general definition of the word—after all, everybody has opinions about something—but rather about the academic expectations of opinion. These include stating one's opinion, supporting opinion through evidence and example, and anticipating and addressing opposing opinions. In elementary school, this is demonstrated through persuasive writing and speech. By middle school, students are challenged to use the more formal structures of argumentation and rhetorical writing, such as Stephen Toulmin's (1958) model of argumentation.

- **Claim:** The position being argued; for example, "Our family should get a dog."

- **Grounds:** The reason given for the claim; answers the question, "What's the proof?" For example, "Dogs have been bred for thousands of years to be good companions and to provide security to their owners."

- **Warrant:** The more formal reasoning or principle that serves as the underpinning for the claim; this links the claim to the grounds; such as, "Many families choose a dog for a pet for these reasons."

- **Backing:** The justification for the warrant; for example, "The Humane Society of the United States says that there are seventy-eight million pet dogs in this country, and 39 percent of all households have at least one dog."

- **Rebuttal:** The counterclaim an opponent might assert; such as, "My parents might worry that they will need to do all the care, but I promise to walk the dog every day."

- **Qualification:** The limits to the claim; for example, "I know I will need help in the beginning because I don't have a lot of experience with dogs. I know I will need to read more about pet care to get really good at it."

The CCSS ELA encourage the purposeful teaching of the elements of argumentation and persuasion to expand students' breadth and depth of formal writing. These rhetorical skills are essential as students progress through middle and high school. Students gain these rhetorical skills as they read and write texts and through small-group discussions and classroom discourse. Perhaps nowhere else in the CCSS ELA will the content knowledge of middle and high school English teachers be more challenged than in designing instruction to prepare students to write for argumentation.

Shift Five: Focus on Academic Vocabulary and Language

A final shift represented in the Common Core standards concerns the development of academic vocabulary and language. As with the other major conceptual changes, this shift's intent is to foster disciplinary links in order to build learning. This approach acknowledges that vocabulary should not be seen as an isolated list of words but rather as labels that we use as a proxy for conceptual understandings. In fact, the language of the standards illuminates this idea. The CCSS note the use of *general academic* and *domain-specific* words and phrases sufficient for reading, writing, speaking and listening, and language (see NGA & CCSSO, 2010a, p. 25). They underscore two key points: (1) academic vocabulary and language entail the use of a broad range of terms (*lexical dexterity*), and (2) vocabulary development extends beyond teaching decontextualized words (NGA & CCSSO, 2010b).

Much of the research underpinning this view of academic vocabulary and language comes from the work of Isabel Beck, Margaret McKeown, and Linda Kucan (2008), whose familiar three-tier model categorizes words and their instruction.

1. **Tier one:** These words are used in everyday speech, are in the vocabulary of most native speakers, and are taught only in the primary grades. However, students who need more language support, such as English learners, will need instruction beyond the first years of schooling. Examples of tier one words include *clock*, *happy*, and *baby* (Beck, McKeown, & Kucan, 2002).

2. **Tier two:** These words (called *general academic words and phrases* in the CCSS) appear more often in texts than in verbal exchanges. For instance, *maintain*, *merchant*, and *benevolent* are examples of tier two words for fourth-grade students (Beck et al., 2002). In addition, tier two words are used in many kinds of texts, not just those that are found within a specific discipline. These words need to be explicitly taught throughout the school years.

3. **Tier three:** These words (called *domain-specific words and phrases* in the CCSS) are closely associated with a specific content and also require specific instruction. Examples of such words at the fourth-grade level include *magnetic field*, *decimals*, and *prime meridian*.

Therefore, an important shift in the Common Core standards concerns the importance of academic language and vocabulary throughout the school day. Special attention should be given to the types of academic language students require in order to express themselves and to understand the writings of others. Furthermore, the rush to profile domain-specific words and phrases can overshadow the importance of general academic vocabulary that students encounter in many kinds of texts. The investment in academic vocabulary and language is well worth it, as vocabulary knowledge is a robust predictor of reading comprehension through eighth grade (Yovanoff, Duesbery, & Alonzo, 2005).

Purposes and Organization of the CCSS ELA

A primary purpose of the CCSS is to prepare students for eventual college and career choices. All schools aspire to successfully prepare students for the future; however, some argue that starting in high school is too late for some students (National Education Goals Panel, 1998). This doesn't mean that elementary and middle school students must start making plans for their adult lives. But insufficient literacy skills do limit one's choices in employment, careers, and postsecondary education. By shining a spotlight on the importance of literacy development across grades K–12, we hope to collectively consider how our 21st century instruction factors into students' lives long after they have left our classrooms.

The Common Core ELA have two sections: (1) language arts standards for grades K–12 and (2) literacy standards in history and social studies, science, and technical subjects for grades 6–12. The language arts standards for grades K–12 are the focus of this book and companion teacher guides in the series *Common Core English Language Arts in a PLC at Work™*. These are the primary standards for teachers of reading and language arts in elementary school (grades K–5) and for teachers of English courses in middle and high school (grades 6–12). The anchor standards for college and career readiness provide the thread that links both the language arts and literacy standards. Although the literacy standards differ by discipline, they are bound by the anchor standards, which articulate the goals for college and career readiness. Anchor standards frame each language arts strand: Reading, Writing, Speaking and Listening, and Language. Figure 2.1 (page 26) explains the different elements of the Common Core State Standards for English language arts.

As noted in figure 2.1, the CCSS spotlight college and career readiness (CCR) with *anchor standards*. Their purpose is to illuminate the college-and-career readiness path. Therefore, anchor standards tie grade-level standards together for kindergartners through graduating seniors. The following principles for college and career readiness shape these anchor standards and describe the growing capabilities of learners as they progress through school. To be college and career ready, students must do the following.

- **Demonstrate independence:** Students must comprehend complex texts in all content areas, participate as speakers and listeners in academic discussions and presentations, direct their own learning, and utilize resources.

- **Build strong content knowledge across all subjects and disciplines:** Cross-discipline knowledge is important for students' writing and discussion. In addition, students should engage in the research and study skills needed to build their content knowledge.

- **Respond to the varying demands of audience, task, purpose, and discipline:** College- and career-ready students communicate in speaking and in writing with a range of audiences and are knowledgeable about the variances of discipline-specific evidence.

Strands are the categories for English language arts in K–5 and 6–12: Reading, Writing, Speaking and Listening, and Language. Additionally, literacy in history and social studies, science, and technical subjects in grades 6–12 focuses on two strands—Reading and Writing.

College and career readiness (CCR) anchor standards define general, cross-disciplinary expectations for reading, writing, speaking and listening, and language. These anchor standards are designated by strand and standard number; for example, R.CCR.6 signifies reading strand (R), anchor standard (CCR), and standard number (six). This standard is from the domain Craft and Structure, which has three standards numbered four, five, and six. The anchor standards are numbered consecutively, one through ten, in the domains.

Domains define categories of CCR anchor standards for each of the strands in the CCSS ELA—Reading, Writing, Speaking and Listening, and Language. For example, four domains are defined for the Writing strand: Text Types and Purposes (standards one, two, and three), Production and Distribution of Writing (standards four, five, and six), Research to Build and Present Knowledge (standards seven, eight, and nine), and Range of Writing (standard ten).

Grade-specific standards define what students should understand and be able to do. The grade-specific standards parallel the CCR anchor standards by translating the broader CCR statements into grade-appropriate end-of-year expectations.

Grade-specific standards are designated by strand, anchor standard, grade level, and standard number; for example, RL.K.1 signifies Reading Standards for Literature (RL), kindergarten level (K), standard one in the domain Key Ideas and Details.

Grade bands are groupings of standards by grade levels—K–2, 3–5, 6–8, 9–10, and 11–12. The grade bands reveal the progression of skills, which are cumulative within and across the grades.

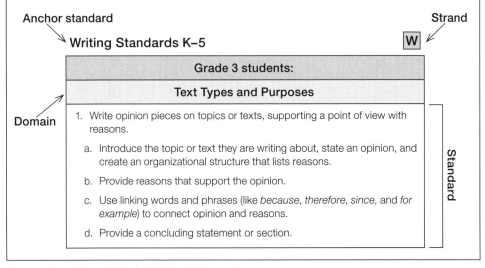

Source: Adapted from NGA & CCSSO, 2010a, p. 20.

Figure 2.1: How to read the CCSS ELA.

- **Comprehend as well as critique:** Students learn this skill as they read and listen to others. They are able to ask questions, evaluate information, and discern reasonableness.

- **Value evidence:** Students should provide evidence in their own oral and written discourse and expect others to furnish evidence.

- **Use technology and digital media strategically and capably:** As they integrate online and offline resources, students should use critical-thinking and communication skills within their digital lives.

- **Understand other perspectives and cultures:** In order to better communicate with and learn from and alongside people, students should understand a wide range of cultural and experiential backgrounds.

The principles and assumptions that guided development of the anchor standards provide a framework for understanding them and their function in girding the grade-level standards. While the CCSS map the territory for literacy development, they do not pretend to describe every aspect of teaching and learning.

Each grade level has its own set of standards that are carefully linked to those that come before and after it. A common mistake that teachers make in discussing the standards is to immediately turn their attention to an individual grade level without first understanding the progression of skills and the role of the grade-specific standards. As NGA and CCSSO (2010a) note, "Students advancing through the grades are expected to meet each year's grade-specific standards and retain or further develop skills and understandings mastered in preceding grades" (p. 11).

The anchor standards, and the grade-specific standards that follow them, are far too complex to teach in a single lesson, or to teach in isolation. As collaborative planning team members examine the Common Core ELA in depth, they should keep this concept in mind. It is the interaction of these standards within and across domains that makes them powerful. To divide and then reassemble them as isolated lessons will undermine the enduring understandings the standards articulate. The overarching goals should be to teach the habits of effective communicators and to avoid isolated strategy instruction (Frey, Fisher, & Berkin, 2008).

In the next sections, we will provide an overview of the anchor standards and domains within each strand—Reading, Writing, Speaking and Listening, and Language. Although ELA teachers will drill down to a greater level of specificity within their collaborative planning teams, it is important for you as a school leader to possess a sense of the content so that you can more fully support their efforts.

Anchor Standards for Reading

There are ten anchor standards for reading organized in the following four domains (see NGA & CCSSO, 2010a, pp. 10, 35).

1. Key Ideas and Details

2. Craft and Structure

3. Integration of Knowledge and Ideas

4. Range of Reading and Level of Text Complexity

These anchor standards are directly tied to two parts within the Reading strand at grades K–12: Literature and Informational Text. Literature is linked to narrative text types—poems, drama, and stories, including folktales, fantasy, and realistic fiction. Although nonfiction biographies and autobiographies often use a narrative structure, they are situated as a type of informational text. The Informational Text standards describe the use of content-rich nonfiction trade books that focus on a concept or topic, biographies and autobiographies, photographic essays, procedural texts, and texts that draw from primary-source documents. The Literature and Informational Text standards for each grade level are drawn directly from the anchor standards (see NGA & CCSSO, 2010a, pp. 11–14, 36–40). A third part, Foundational Skills, is specific to K–5 only; it is the only one that does not have a set of anchor standards, because they are not outcome standards, but rather necessary prerequisite skills for emergent, early, and intermediate readers. These skills require students to have phonemic awareness, alphabetic knowledge, and phonological knowledge to succeed in middle and high school (see NGA & CCSSO, 2010a, pp. 15–17).

Key Ideas and Details

The three anchor standards in this domain contain many expected elements, as well as some more challenging demands that have implications for instruction.

1. Read closely to determine what the text says explicitly and to make logical inferences from it; cite specific textual evidence when writing or speaking to support conclusions drawn from the text. (R.CCR.1)

2. Determine central ideas or themes of a text and analyze their development; summarize the key supporting details and ideas. (R.CCR.2)

3. Analyze how and why individuals, events, and ideas develop and interact over the course of a text. (R.CCR.3) (NGA & CCSSO, 2010a, pp. 10, 35)

In order for students to achieve these goals, they will need instruction that includes text-dependent questions designed to elicit such information. These questions encourage readers to look back into the text to locate information. A likely area of support teachers will require is in developing the habit of asking text-dependent questions throughout their lessons.

Craft and Structure

The three anchor standards in this domain focus on the reader's ability to analyze texts at the micro and macro levels to determine how author's word choice, organizational structure, and point of view form the content and style of the text.

4. Interpret words and phrases as they are used in a text, including determining technical, connotative, and figurative meanings, and analyze how specific word choices shape meaning or tone. (R.CCR.4)

5. Analyze the structure of texts, including how specific sentences, paragraphs, and larger portions of the text (e.g., a section, chapter, scene, or stanza) relate to each other and the whole. (R.CCR.5)

6. Assess how point of view or purpose shapes the content and style of a text. (R.CCR.6) (NGA & CCSSO, 2010a, pp. 10, 35)

You can see the role vocabulary plays in these standards. In addition, across the grade levels, students are deepening their understanding of point of view, first from their own standpoint, then from the angle of the characters they encounter. A possible area of additional support that some teachers may need is developing a habit of querying the author's purposes in the texts they read and discuss.

Integration of Knowledge and Ideas

Only two of the three anchor standards for this domain appear in the Literature part of the Reading strand, as argumentation in anchor standard eight (R.CCR.8) is not commonly utilized in fiction. This domain highlights the importance of being able to extract and synthesize information from a variety of internal and external sources.

7. Integrate and evaluate content presented in diverse media and formats, including visually and quantitatively, as well as in words. (R.CCR.7)

8. Delineate and evaluate the argument and specific claims in a text, including the validity of the reasoning as well as the relevance and sufficiency of the evidence. (R.CCR.8)

9. Analyze how two or more texts address similar themes or topics in order to build knowledge or to compare the approaches the authors take. (R.CCR.9) (NGA & CCSSO, 2010a, pp. 10, 35)

Anchor standard seven's (R.CCR.7) focus on visual literacy is likely to represent a genuine departure from what most educators teach. While extraction of information from illustrations is common in the primary grades, the dominance of text in the middle school and high school often means that this form of literacy is often neglected. By fifth grade, multiliteracies take a front seat: movement, light, sound, and images are the elements that comprise multimodal presentations (Frey, Fisher, & Gonzalez, 2010). Because this anchor standard presents teachers with new challenges, you should watch for supports they may need to more fully understand visual literacies and how to teach the necessary skills.

Anchor standard seven (R.CCR.7) is an example of the interrelationships among the domains in other strands. For example, anchor standard seven is closely tied to the Writing anchor standard domain Research to Build and Present Knowledge (see NGA & CCSSO, 2010a, pp. 18, 41), as well as the Speaking and Listening domain Comprehension and Collaboration (see NGA & CCSSO, 2010a, pp. 22, 48).

Range of Reading and Level of Text Complexity

Anchor standard ten (R.CCR.10) is brief but heavily influences much of the instruction across all the strands and their standards.

> 10. Read and comprehend complex literary and informational texts independently and proficiently. (R.CCR.10) (NGA & CCSSO, 2010a, pp. 10, 35)

One can see how text complexity and scaffolded instruction intersect, as there is language throughout the grade-specific standards that references this practice, noting at times that students are receiving adult support or reading independently at the high end of the range of text complexity.

Text complexity is defined across three dimensions: (1) quantitative measures, (2) qualitative factors, and (3) reader and task considerations. Quantitative measures, using a mixture of word length, sentence length, and syllables, are familiar to educators. In addition, many readability formulae calculate the number of difficult words that appear in a text by comparing these to grade-level lists. Examples of quantitative measures include the Fry Readability Formula, Dale-Chall Readability Formula, and Flesch-Kincaid Grade-Level Index (see Fisher, Frey, & Lapp, 2012), as well as commercial ones such as ATOS (used by Accelerated Reader), Source Rater (Educational Testing Service), Pearson Reading Maturity Scale (Pearson Education), Degrees of Reading Power (Questar), and Lexile (MetaMetrics). Published quantitative reading scores can provide a platform for collaborative teams to begin to examine texts to use with their students.

The Lexile measures used in the CCSS have been revised, which may create a potential area of confusion for teachers. The new recommended text levels shown in table 2.2 differ from the originals provided in appendix A of the Common Core ELA (see NGA & CCSSO, 2010b, p. 8). For example, the original range for the grades 2–3 band was 450–720L, compared to the revised range of 420–820L. These were revised at the suggestion of many professional groups, and the new bands have been widened to reflect a broader range of readers, especially in the primary grades. Be sure that collaborative planning teams are working with updated information regarding text complexity.

Table 2.2: Text Complexity Ranges Within Grade Bands

Grade Band	Revised CCSS 2011	Accelerated Reader	Degrees of Reading Power	Flesch-Kincaid	Source Rater	Reading Maturity Scale
K–1	n/a	n/a	n/a	n/a	n/a	n/a
2–3	420–820	2.75–5.14	42–54	1.98–5.34	0.05–2.48	3.53–6.13
4–5	740–1010	4.97–7.03	52–60	4.51–7.73	0.84–5.75	5.42–7.92
6–8	925–1185	7.00–9.98	57–67	6.51–10.34	4.11–10.66	7.04–9.57
9–10	1050–1335	9.67–12.01	62–72	8.32–12.12	9.02–13.93	8.41–10.81
11–CCR	1185–1385	11.20–14.10	67–74	10.34–14.20	12.30–14.50	9.57–12.00

Source: CCSSO, 2012a.

Anchor Standards for Writing

The college- and career-ready anchor standards for writing were designed to articulate the need for a strong foundation across disciplines, audiences, and purposes. Writing, like speaking, is a form of communication. However, two important differences exist: the audience is often unseen, and the product is often permanent. The fact is that we judge others by what they write and how they say it. Too many misspellings and we wonder whether the person is careless. We assume disorganized discourse is the product of a jumbled mind. We often dismiss opinions altogether if there is nothing to back up the claims. In each case, the writer may be careful, organized, and articulate, but writing may fail him or her. The anchor standards are an effort to ensure that students are able to communicate effectively in written form in order to represent themselves in the classroom, workplace, and world. There are ten anchor standards for writing, extending from kindergarten through twelfth grade.

The ten anchor standards for writing are organized into four domains (see NGA & CCSSO, 2010a, pp. 18, 41).

1. Text Types and Purposes

2. Production and Distribution of Writing

3. Research to Build and Present Knowledge

4. Range of Writing

Text Types and Purposes

This domain has three anchor standards (W.CCR.1, 2, and 3), which define three major types of writing that are tied to their purposes—writing for argumentation, writing to inform or explain, and writing to convey real or imagined experiences. These basic text types are expressed through many writing genres, which in themselves are often a blend of two or more text types. For example, an opinion piece may include elements of argument, as well as narrative to describe the writer's perspective. Therefore, these should not be viewed too narrowly as a mandate to teach only three writing genres. Rather, it is an important reminder that we need to clearly link purposes for writing, not just the format for a genre.

1. Write arguments to support claims in an analysis of substantive topics or texts, using valid reasoning and relevant and sufficient evidence. (W.CCR.1)

2. Write informative/explanatory texts to examine and convey complex ideas and information clearly and accurately through the effective selection, organization, and analysis of content. (W.CCR.2)

3. Write narratives to develop real or imagined experiences or events using effective technique, well-chosen details, and well-structured event sequences. (W.CCR.3) (NGA & CCSSO, 2010a, pp. 18, 41)

Production and Distribution of Writing

This domain focuses on the communicative nature of writing. Anchor standard four (W.CCR.4) encourages teachers to link the task, purpose, and audience to the selected genre or format. In anchor standard six (W.CCR.6), we see how writing is lifted from a solitary and isolated act to one that involves peers, fellow writers, teachers, and experts across the classroom, community, and world. Anchor standard five (W.CCR.5) bridges the other two anchor standards in this domain, articulating the processes a writer must necessarily engage with in order to communicate effectively.

4. Produce clear and coherent writing in which the development, organization, and style are appropriate to task, purpose, and audience. (W.CCR.4)

5. Develop and strengthen writing as needed by planning, revising, editing, rewriting, or trying a new approach. (W.CCR.5)

6. Use technology, including the Internet, to produce and publish writing and to interact and collaborate with others. (W.CCR.6) (NGA & CCSSO, 2010a, pp. 18, 41)

Research to Build and Present Knowledge

This domain foregrounds the importance of academic writing in its three anchor standards (W.CCR.7, 8, and 9). Learners are encouraged to gather information from a variety of sources in order to investigate topics of worth. The topics should be a natural extension of the learning students engage in across their academic career—not just as consumers of information, but also as users and producers of the same. This requires that students critically analyze information sources, both literary and informational, and use the analysis in their writing to conduct inquiry and research.

7. Conduct short as well as more sustained research projects based on focused questions, demonstrating understanding of the subject under investigation. (W.CCR.7)

8. Gather relevant information from multiple print and digital sources, assess the credibility and accuracy of each source, and integrate the information while avoiding plagiarism. (W.CCR.8)

9. Draw evidence from literary or informational texts to support analysis, reflection, and research. (W.CCR.9) (NGA & CCSSO, 2010a, pp. 18, 41)

Range of Writing

Routinely is the key word in anchor standard ten (W.CCR.10). Writing is not something that is done only occasionally, but daily, and for extended periods of time in order to increase volume. As with reading, the intent is to build skill and stamina through frequent application and practice.

10. Write routinely over extended time frames (time for research, reflection, and revision) and shorter time frames (a single sitting or a day or two) for a range of tasks, purposes, and audiences. (W.CCR.10) (NGA & CCSSO, 2010a, pp. 18, 41)

Teachers may require additional support in implementing the Writing standards, including professional development targeted at developing consensus scoring skills and recognizing and teaching argumentation. Some teachers may also need assistance in restructuring writing curricula so they focus more on writing with other texts in mind, rather than predominately on personal response writing. Observing how students are developing as writers is an important aspect of teaching writing well. The Common Core ELA contains a collection of student writing samples that you may want to examine with your teachers in collaborative team meetings to help them understand the progression of writing skill across grade bands. Featured in appendix C of the CCSS (NGA & CCSSO, 2010c), these writing samples reflect a range of writing ability and were constructed under several conditions, including on-demand writing, as well as more polished pieces that were developed through several rounds of editing and revision.

Anchor Standards for Speaking and Listening

The Speaking and Listening anchor standards spotlight the quality of transactions students have across the table, classroom, and world. NGA and CCSSO (2010a) note, "Students must have ample opportunities to take part in a variety of rich, structured conversations—as part of a whole class, in small groups, and with a partner" (p. 22). In the 21st century, in which digital communications have become a feature of everyday life, these communication skills extend to virtual environments.

The anchor standards for speaking and listening are divided into two domains (see NGA & CCSSO, 2010a, pp. 22, 48).

1. Comprehension and Collaboration

2. Presentation of Knowledge and Ideas

Together, they outline the expectations for the informal and formal talk of an effective classroom. Notice how these standards clearly link to those discussed in the Reading and Writing strands (see pages 27 and 31 in this chapter).

Comprehension and Collaboration

The three anchor standards in this domain focus on the student's growing ability to collaborate with others in a meaningful way, using the content as the platform for his or her work. Anchor standard one (SL.CCR.1) describes the dispositions of the student who is fully prepared to participate in academic discussions. Anchor standard three (SL.CCR.3) is reminiscent of the work on accountable talk, which describes the habits of speakers and listeners as they engage in academic discourse, such as incorporating the statements of others into the discussion, asking questions, using evidence and examples, and even disagreeing with one another (Michaels, O'Connor, & Resnick, 2008). Anchor standard two (SL.CCR.2) bridges the other two anchor standards by specifying the role that content knowledge plays in these conversations.

1. Prepare for and participate effectively in a range of conversations and collaborations with diverse partners, building on others' ideas and expressing their own clearly and persuasively. (SL.CCR.1)

2. Integrate and evaluate information presented in diverse media and formats, including visually, quantitatively, and orally. (SL.CCR.2)

3. Evaluate a speaker's point of view, reasoning, and use of evidence and rhetoric. (SL.CCR.3) (NGA & CCSSO, 2010a, pp. 22, 48)

Presentation of Knowledge and Ideas

The second domain of anchor standards for the Speaking and Listening strand profiles the essential nature of presenting information to one another in more formal ways. Anchor standard four (SL.CCR.4) discusses the ways a speaker organizes and presents information, always keeping the audience and the purpose for the presentation in mind. Anchor standard six (SL.CCR.6) is a reminder that presenters are also listeners and consumers of information. As such, they need to use critical-thinking skills in order to make judgments about the information being shared. Anchor standard five (SL.CCR.5) serves to bridge these two ideas and focuses on the presenter's skills in using digital media and visual displays of information, as well as the listener's ability to understand it.

4. Present information, findings, and supporting evidence such that listeners can follow the line of reasoning and the organization, development, and style are appropriate to task, purpose, and audience. (SL.CCR.4)

5. Make strategic use of digital media and visual displays of data to express information and enhance understanding of presentations. (SL.CCR.5)

6. Adapt speech to a variety of contexts and communicative tasks, demonstrating command of formal English when indicated or appropriate. (SL.CCR.6) (NGA & CCSSO, 2010a, pp. 22, 48)

Taken together, the anchor standards for speaking and listening highlight the integral role of peers in the learning process. Long gone is the notion that all knowledge emanates from the teacher and that the student's chief role is to listen quietly and take it all in (Frey et al., 2009). Peer learning has become a dominant feature in 21st century classrooms, which carries implications for how teachers enable students to interact. These standards are not about being able to pass on pleasantries to one another; they are the engine of learning. As a school leader, you may need to provide teachers with additional professional development on methods for promoting interaction and student talk in the classroom. Additionally, remind teachers that you anticipate hearing student voices throughout the day, ensuring them you do not expect classrooms to be silent.

Anchor Standards for Language

A final set of the Common Core ELA standards is dedicated to language. Speech and language are closely related, but they do have distinct features that make them unique. Speech concerns verbal expression; language describes what words mean (vocabulary), how they are strung together to make sense using the rules of the language (grammar and syntax), how new words are made (conjugation), and what word combinations work best for a specific situation (pragmatics and register) (American Speech-Language-Hearing

Association, 2012). Language is foundational to what we do—it's integral to our behavior. Consequently, it can be difficult to distance ourselves from it in order to observe it. As the saying goes, "The last thing a fish notices is the water it swims in." Language is to humans as water is to fish. By the way, your ability to understand that last idiom and its analogy speaks to your command of language. The NGA and CCSSO (2010a) put it a different way:

> The inclusion of Language standards in their own strand should not be taken as an indication that skills related to conventions, effective language use, and vocabulary are unimportant to reading, writing, speaking, and listening; indeed, they are inseparable from such contexts. (p. 25)

The overall intent of the Language standards speaks to the need to raise our students' awareness of language, which is something they are not likely to be able to master without an aware teacher's intentional instruction.

The six anchor standards for language are organized in three domains (see NGA & CCSSO, 2010a, pp. 25, 51).

1. Conventions of Standard English

2. Knowledge of Language

3. Vocabulary Acquisition and Use

Conventions of Standard English

This first domain of standards concerns itself with the grammatical rules of spoken and written language, especially as they pertain to parts of speech, written conventions, and spelling. These are essential to communication and involve issues related to the development of complex sentences, as well as voice and mood.

> 1. Demonstrate command of the conventions of standard English grammar and usage when writing or speaking. (L.CCR.1)
>
> 2. Demonstrate command of the conventions of standard English capitalization, punctuation, and spelling when writing. (L.CCR.2) (NGA & CCSSO, 2010a, pp. 25, 51)

Knowledge of Language

This domain has a single anchor standard that covers quite a bit of territory. Beginning in grade 2 (there isn't a grade-level standard for this domain in kindergarten or first grade), students begin to attend to the registers of language, especially in comparing formal and informal modes. By high school, students are applying their knowledge of language through the use of style guides, like Modern Language Association (MLA) style. This anchor standard is strongly linked to those in Writing (for example, W.CCR.4) and in Speaking and Listening (for example, SL.CCR.4).

> 3. Apply knowledge of language to understand how language functions in different contexts, to make effective choices for meaning or style, and to comprehend more fully when reading or listening. (L.CCR.3) (NGA & CCSSO, 2010a, pp. 25, 51)

Vocabulary Acquisition and Use

This domain has received significant attention in the educational community because of the emphasis on word solving in anchor standard four (L.CCR.4). While this approach to vocabulary development has been widely researched (for example, Baumann, Font, Edwards, & Boland, 2005; Blachowicz & Fisher, 2002), in practice there has been a more prominent focus on lists of words. As anchor standard six (L.CCR.6) illustrates, grade-level vocabulary lists are valuable. Every teacher should have a strong sense of the grade-level vocabulary expectations. However, this should be coupled with purposeful instruction on how to solve for unknown words.

A second area of attention has been on the nuanced use of language in anchor standard six. Note that it defines vocabulary as *words and phrases*, not single words alone. In addition, it describes these words and phrases as *general academic* and *domain specific*. These terms align with the work of Beck et al. (2002) and their description of tier two words (in the language of CCSS, they are general academic words and phrases like *motionless* and *endearing qualities*) that mature language users use in several contexts. In addition, tier three words are those domain-specific words and phrases that are tied to a discipline, like using *nebula* and *recessive genes* in science. Anchor standard five (L.CCR.5) draws attention to the need to appreciate the artistry of words that convey just the right meaning, tone, and mood.

4. Determine or clarify the meaning of unknown and multiple-meaning words and phrases by using context clues, analyzing meaningful word parts, and consulting general and specialized reference materials, as appropriate. (L.CCR.4)

5. Demonstrate understanding of figurative language, word relationships, and nuances in word meanings. (L.CCR.5)

6. Acquire and use accurately a range of general academic and domain-specific words and phrases sufficient for reading, writing, speaking, and listening at the college and career readiness level; demonstrate independence in gathering vocabulary knowledge when encountering an unknown term important to comprehension or expression. (L.CCR.6) (NGA & CCSSO, 2010a, pp. 25, 51)

Note that in grades 6–12, L.CCR.6 is a bit different. It reads "Acquire and use accurately a range of general academic and domain-specific words and phrases sufficient for reading, writing, speaking, and listening at the college and career readiness level; demonstrate independence in gathering vocabulary knowledge when *considering a word or phrase* important to comprehension or expression." Grades 6–12 students should already have practice with word solving and be able to use this habit.

The anchor standards frame a pathway for language development from kindergarten through twelfth grade, with an eye toward systematically preparing students for the language demands of college and careers. When supporting teachers in their collaborative planning groups, listen for possible confusions students have about language concepts and how they are evidenced in reading, writing, speaking, and listening. Additionally, teachers may need support in developing a robust vocabulary program that spans several grade levels. For example, they may need time and materials for preparing a cohesive schoolwide vocabulary program that highlights general academic and domain-specific words and phrases.

Conclusion

This chapter provided you as a school leader with an overview of the Common Core State Standards for English language arts. While teachers will be working more closely on understanding the curricular implications of the standards, it is essential for school leaders to possess a working knowledge of the content and organization. The companion titles in the *Common Core English Language Arts in a PLC at Work™* series are designed to support your efforts in facilitating the necessary, fine-grained analyses of the standards in collaborative planning teams.

As a review, the Common Core State Standards for English language arts are organized across four strands: Reading, Writing, Speaking and Listening, and Language. College and career anchor standards for grades K–12 frame each strand. These anchor standards articulate the overarching goals that shape the grade-specific standards and were designed to create a progression across elementary, middle, and high school. This integrated, multigrade-level framework intends to reduce the *silo effect* that can creep into education and limit teachers to working in isolation from their peers with an uncoordinated curriculum. While students and their families experience schooling as a growth process extending across grade levels and buildings, the traditional organizational structures of schools often work at odds with this sense of continuity. By viewing learning experiences in a progressive manner across grade bands and buildings, we can begin to mirror more closely the experiences of our students and their families. The anchor standards are an attempt to foster communication and action across educational systems.

CHAPTER 3

Leading the Implementation of High-Quality Instruction

KEY QUESTIONS

- How do you define *high-quality instruction*? To what extent do you think teachers in your school or district share this definition? What discussions have you had with faculty about the features of high-quality instruction?

- What challenges do your teachers face in accommodating students' diverse learning needs? How have you helped teachers deal with these challenges?

- What features do you look for in your school's literacy programs? Which features are consistent within and across grade levels? What do you think are the strengths of the school's literacy program? What are its limitations?

The Common Core State Standards for English language arts represent the content—the *what* of teaching. Understanding what students are expected to learn is an important aspect of schooling. If teachers teach the wrong content, students will not achieve as expected. For example, if a seventh-grade teacher provides an excellent year of high-quality instruction using fifth-grade standards, the students will exit the year as incoming eighth graders ready for sixth grade. This is a challenging point as many teachers focus on students' development and teach to their current level of performance. As a leader, you will need to monitor the content teachers deliver and guide them to raise their expectations for all students. The focus of the previous chapter, understanding the CCSS, is a critical first step.

The Importance of Shared Understandings

In the absence of sound instruction, curriculum alone is insufficient to improve student achievement. Documents will not teach a student how to resolve unknown words, collaborate with peers on a digital project, or consider the carefully constructed arguments of an author. The rigorous content of the Common Core ELA must be matched with vigorous teaching. You will need to lead the implementation of high-quality instruction—the *how* of teaching—to ensure that teaching is invigorated. This is likely to be more difficult than leading the *what* of teaching. Leading both the what and how of teaching is what distinguishes an instructional leader from a building manager.

Implementation of the CCSS will require instructional leadership. That's not to say that managing the building is not important; however, *leaders* assume responsibility for the instructional program.

Administrators and teacher leaders must complete a number of tasks, ranging from lunchtime supervision to budgets to discipline of students—all necessary to keep a school operating. Unfortunately, for many educational leaders, pressing responsibilities related to school operations take precedence and interfere with their ability to serve as instructional leaders. As a result, they are prevented from spending time observing classroom instruction and talking with teachers about their professional practice.

Getting leaders into classrooms is important if school improvement efforts are to flourish. As school leaders spend time in classrooms, providing feedback and modeling high-quality instructional practice, they must also reach agreement with teachers on what constitutes quality instruction. Shared understandings about quality lay the foundation for productive conversations about the contents of a lesson. (See chapter 5, page 75, for more on this point.) Our experiences with school improvement efforts suggest that agreements on quality are crucial to the effectiveness of professional development and administrative or peer feedback. Defining and agreeing on high-quality instruction should be a skill that instructional leaders practice regularly.

Principal Ted Williams just returned from a conference that validated and extended his understanding of the importance of building on students' background knowledge in lessons. He is observing the classroom instruction of fifth-grade teacher Leona Filippo. As part of his observation, he notices several opportunities that Ms. Filippo missed to build and activate background knowledge.

"How do you think the lesson went?" Principal Williams asks after class.

"Great, I thought that my students were all engaged," Ms. Filippo replies.

"Yes, true, they all seemed interested in the topic," Principal Williams notes. "Did you think about what they might already know about the topic? Or what they might not know about the topic?" he questions.

Ms. Filippo thinks and responds, "No, not really. I think that they learned a lot from the experience. Did you hear them talking with each other?"

"Yes, they were talking and asking good questions," Principal Williams admits. "But what did they already know?"

"I'm not sure," she replies. "But I will bet that they do well on the assessment."

Principal Williams asks, "Did you think about making connections between their background knowledge and the topic at hand? Could it be that some of the students already knew this before the lesson?"

"Sure," Ms. Filippo says, "but that's what happens in every lesson. Some know it already, some get it, and others need more teaching."

Principal Williams notes, "I think it would be useful to tap into students' background knowledge and then build on that with students."

"Yeah, maybe," she says. "I really liked the summaries they wrote at the end. You didn't get to see that part, but I can show you what they wrote. See [*handing Principal Williams some student work*]?"

This conversation isn't really getting anywhere because Principal Williams and Ms. Filippo have a different understanding of quality, at least in terms of the topic of background knowledge. As a result, Ms. Filippo is immune to the feedback being provided and is not likely to change as a result of the experience. Reaching agreement on quality is a top priority for effective leaders. Shared understandings about quality instruction provide a baseline from which a meaningful conversation can be had and changes can be addressed.

Components of High-Quality Instruction

First proposed in 1983, the gradual release of responsibility model of instruction suggests that cognitive work should shift slowly and intentionally from the teacher as model, to joint responsibility between teachers and students, and finally to a learner's independent practice and application (Pearson & Gallagher, 1983). The gradual release of responsibility model of instruction provides a structure for the teacher to move from assuming "all the responsibility for performing a task . . . to a situation in which the students assume all of the responsibility" (Duke & Pearson, 2002, p. 211).

The gradual release of responsibility model of instruction is built on several theories, including:

- Jean Piaget's (1952) work on cognitive structures and schema

- Lev Vygotsky's (1962, 1978) work on zones of proximal development

- Albert Bandura's (1965) work on attention, retention, reproduction, and motivation

- David Wood, Jerome Bruner, and Gail Ross's (1976) work on scaffolded instruction

Taken together, these theories suggest that students learn through interactions with others; when these interactions are intentional, specific learning occurs. The gradual release of responsibility model has four components for high-quality instruction (Fisher & Frey, 2008).

1. **Purpose and modeling:** The teacher establishes the purpose of the lesson focusing on what students are expected to *learn*, not what they are expected to *do* (Fisher & Frey, 2011). The purpose should be based on the expected learning outcomes, such as standards, and be clearly communicated to students. In addition, a high-quality purpose statement should connect the learner to life outside the classroom, provide the learner an opportunity to

learn something about himself or herself, and be part of a worthy body of college- and career-ready knowledge. Through modeling of the purpose, the teacher shares his or her thinking. Teacher modeling should provide students with an example of the critical thinking and academic language required to be successful (Fisher, Frey, & Lapp, 2008). In addition, modeling should be meta-cognitive in nature, meaning that students understand how the teacher thought about the topic and not just what the teacher thought about the topic.

2. **Guided instruction:** The teacher strategically uses questions, prompts, and cues to facilitate student understanding (Fisher & Frey, 2010). This can be done with whole groups of students but is probably more effective with small groups that are composed based on instructional needs. During guided instruction, the teacher focuses on releasing responsibility to students while providing instructional scaffolds to ensure that students are successful.

3. **Productive group work:** Students work in collaborative groups to produce something related to the topic at hand (Frey et al., 2009). To be productive, the group work must involve students using academic language and being individually accountable for their contribution to the effort. This phase of instruction should provide students with an opportunity to consolidate their understanding before applying it independently.

4. **Independent learning:** Students apply what they have learned in class and outside of class. Many independent learning tasks are used as formative assessments, designed to check for understanding and to identify needs for reteaching. Of course, independent learning tasks should not come too soon in the instructional cycle as students need practice before applying knowledge in new situations.

Figure 3.1 shows the relationships among these components and the transition between teacher responsibility and student responsibility.

The components in the gradual release of responsibility model of instruction can be used in any order as long as they are included in every lesson.

For example, ninth-grade English teacher Rebecca Calhoun starts an informational text unit with a journal entry prompt designed to activate students' background knowledge (independent learning). She then asks students to discuss their responses with a partner (productive group work) and add notes from their partner to their journal page. Next, she establishes the purpose and models her thinking while reading from the informational text (purpose and modeling). With this added information, she asks the partners to join with another pair to form a group of four. Together, the students create a collaborative poster synthesizing and summarizing their understanding of the question (productive group work). Students write with different color markers on the poster for individual accountability and talk about what they are writing (independent learning). As they do so, she moves around the room checking for understanding (guided instruction). Students

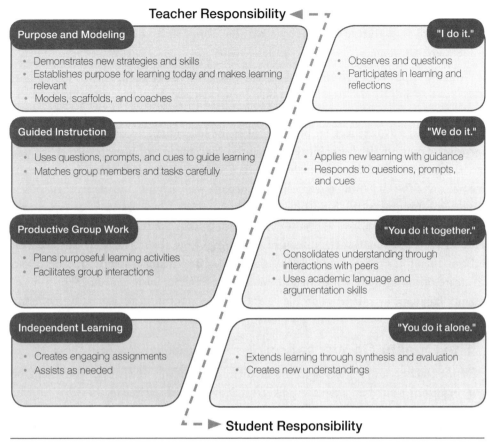

Teacher Responsibility ◄ – ┐

Purpose and Modeling

- Demonstrates new strategies and skills
- Establishes purpose for learning today and makes learning relevant
- Models, scaffolds, and coaches

"I do it."

- Observes and questions
- Participates in learning and reflections

Guided Instruction

- Uses questions, prompts, and cues to guide learning
- Matches group members and tasks carefully

"We do it."

- Applies new learning with guidance
- Responds to questions, prompts, and cues

Productive Group Work

- Plans purposeful learning activities
- Facilitates group interactions

"You do it together."

- Consolidates understanding through interactions with peers
- Uses academic language and argumentation skills

Independent Learning

- Creates engaging assignments
- Assists as needed

"You do it alone."

- Extends learning through synthesis and evaluation
- Creates new understandings

Student Responsibility ►

Figure 3.1: Instructional framework based on the gradual release of responsibility model of instruction.

Visit **go.solution-tree.com/commoncore** for a reproducible version of this figure.

in her class know that she will stop by and ask them about what they've written so they refrain from writing something that they don't understand. They talk to their teammates to ensure that they understand the content before they commit to their responses in writing. When Ms. Calhoun stops by one of the groups, she notices that the students have included incorrect information on their poster. She asks about this information and then provides the group with a prompt to encourage critical thinking about the incorrect information (guided instruction). When this does not result in understanding, she cues the students to re-read a specific paragraph of the text, which leads them to understand their mistake and correct it.

The gradual release of responsibility model of instruction includes direct, explicit instruction, as well as guided instruction as students try tasks themselves. Students gradually assume more responsibility for using the skill or strategy as they work with one another as well as on their own. In high-quality English language arts instruction, the teacher initially controls the reading and writing through direct instruction in focus lessons. Students assume more control during guided instruction. Teachers introduce and refine skills during direct instruction and guided instruction and have students practice with peers during collaborative learning. These skills then become part of each student's repertoire of skills in independent learning.

Despite the power of this model of instruction, it will not be successful without connections to the learners' lives. Meaningful experiences enhance learning because the student can apply the new knowledge to a familiar situation. A basic premise of learning is that when experiences are meaningful to the individual, his or her ability to learn increases. For example, your ability to learn the concepts in this book is directly related to the relevancy of the material to your life. If you are responsible for leading the implementation of the CCSS in your grade level, department, school, or district, this book is likely a meaningful addition to your professional library. When learners have questions for which they need answers, reading and writing tasks are increasingly meaningful. Furthermore, learning is social in nature and springs from the interactions we have with others. Therefore, an important role of the teacher is to foster students' questions and to create meaningful activities that allow them to interact with one another. In high-quality language arts instruction, skills and strategies introduced as part of modeling are practiced and extended through guided, collaborative, and independent learning.

The Quality Conversation

When teachers and leaders agree on quality and examine student performance, the conversations that they have are powerful. As we noted earlier in this chapter, the absence of an agreement on quality or the lack of focus on student learning results in conversations that do not impact practice.

Eleventh-grade teacher Seeta Patil develops an agreement of key quality indicators with Principal Consuela Ramirez related to productive group work for lessons. For example, the teachers at her school are focused on complexity of the task because their student performance data suggest that students are not being challenged. They also focus on individual accountability during group learning because some of the student work appears to be copied from peers. Consequently, their conversation about lesson observations is much more productive and likely to result in changes. Unlike the first conversation in this chapter (see page 40) between Ms. Filippo and Principal Williams, in which there was not a shared definition of quality, this conversation results in reflection and growth.

After a lesson on understanding author's purpose, Ms. Patil discusses Principal Ramirez's observations.

"I think that the students understood the purpose," says Ms. Patil. "Did you understand it?"

"Yes, even though I wasn't an English teacher, I understood what you were expecting me to learn from the lesson," Principal Ramirez replies. "I appreciated the fact that you defined key terms as you established the purpose. But let's talk about what happened before the purpose, OK?"

"Sure," Ms. Patil says. "I really wanted to get students talking right away. I felt like the independent task worked and that their partner conversations helped them clarify some information."

"I agree that it was useful to the students. How was it, if at all, useful to you?" Principal Ramirez asks.

"I'm not sure what you mean," Ms. Patil says.

"Did you use any of the information from the independent task and first productive group work later in the lesson?" Principal Ramirez asks.

Ms. Patil says, "I kept it in mind, but I think I know where you're going. I've told you that I would like to improve my differentiated instruction, and I think that my modeling might have been more focused on what I heard students saying."

"That's something to think about," Principal Ramirez says. "Do you think students learned something important today?"

"Yes, I really do," Ms. Patil replies. "Their collaborative posters really showed me which parts of the purpose they got and which I need to keep focused on."

"And I have to say that your ability to guide learning through prompts and cues is impressive," Principal Ramirez says. "It seems effortless as you help students reach new levels of understanding. I know it's not, but you make it seem so."

"Thanks. I think that I'd like to try modeling in that lesson a bit differently. Can you come to my last period class and see the difference?" Ms. Patil asks.

"Sure! I'd love to be there," Principal Ramirez replies.

Quality Agreements in Practice

Principals and teachers can make agreements about quality at the school or even the district level. When principals and teachers collaborate on quality, observations and feedback are useful in guiding their conversations. Agreement over quality is a powerful first step in improving student achievement. In addition to the conversations these agreements foster, they can be used as a type of needs assessment for additional professional development. For example, the staff at a local high school agree on specific quality indicators for each component of the gradual release of responsibility model of instruction (see table 3.1, page 46). These indicators guide the work of collaborative planning teams, which results in them identifying specific topics for additional professional development.

Table 3.1: Sample Quality Indicators for Gradual Release of Responsibility Model of Instruction

High-Quality Component	Indicator
Purpose and Modeling	Teachers explicitly present *purpose* through content and language goals, which are based on content standards and the language demands of the task, as well as students' needs identified via formative assessments.
	Modeling includes naming the task or strategy, explaining when it is used, and using analogies to link to new learning. Teachers demonstrate the task or strategy, alert learners about errors to avoid, and show them how to check for accuracy. The modeling consistently contains "I" statements.
Guided Instruction	Teachers use questions, prompts, and cues to guide students to greater understanding and do not provide students with direct explanations unless the prompts and cues fail to result in understanding.
	When students are in small groups, teachers base guided instruction on an assessed instructional need and not an artificial performance level.
Productive Group Work	The task is a novel application of a grade-level-appropriate concept and is designed so that the success is not guaranteed. A chance for productive failure exists such that students remain challenged and engaged in the task at hand.
	Teachers purposefully construct small groups of two to five students (heterogeneous grouping) to maximize individual strengths without magnifying areas of need.
Independent Learning	The task is a novel application that relates to purpose of the lesson and provides students with an opportunity to apply what they have learned.
	Students practice with their peers before teachers ask them to complete tasks independently.
	Teachers and school leaders use student responses to independent tasks to make future instructional decisions, such as whole-class reteaching or additional guided instruction.

Visit **go.solution-tree.com/commoncore** for a reproducible version of this table.

When the teachers at this school focus on implementing the quality indicators, they are interested in hearing what their peers and leaders think. This common language facilitates conversations between and among teachers and provides a reason for them to plan together and observe each other. They are no longer impervious to feedback, but rather open to it as an opportunity to make additional changes in their instructional repertoires. Over time, the teachers and leaders add additional quality indicators as they notice factors they think should be implemented schoolwide. Through quality agreements in practice, the achievement at this school soared, and it's now one of the highest achieving schools in the area. Improvement comes when teachers and leaders agree on quality and start having meaningful conversations about teaching and learning. As Aristotle noted, "Quality is not an act, it is a habit." That's what agreements on quality create: habits that teachers use to ensure student understanding.

With the gradual release of responsibility model of instruction in mind, and a focus on reaching agreements about high-quality instruction, you are ready to tackle some of the big challenges that interfere with achievement in the English language arts classroom, including effective grouping structures, supports for English learners and students with special needs, and effective ELA programs.

Effective Grouping Structures

How teachers group students for instruction matters a great deal. Specifically, *permanent ability grouping* has a harmful effect on the classroom community. When teachers group students by perceived ability and do not change groups or make them flexible, students often become stagnant and lose confidence in their abilities. This practice not only disrupts the sense of community that students enjoy but also negatively impacts student achievement, particularly among students who struggle to achieve (Broussard & Joseph, 1998; Mallery & Mallery, 1999). Students who experience permanent ability groups report less satisfaction with school and believe they are failures (Boaler, William, & Brown, 2000). Robert Slavin and Jomills Braddock (1993) further suggest that permanent ability grouping not only harms academic and social constructs but also undermines the democratic values of the United States that encourage individuals to rise above adversity and participate in their citizenship. In terms of the Common Core, permanent ability grouping fails to encourage students to interact with a wide range of people—people they may meet in college or in the workplace.

High-quality English language arts instruction relies on a number of flexible grouping patterns. These patterns include whole-class guided learning in which the teacher asks students questions, prompts, and cues; small-group guided learning in which the teacher targets the questions, prompts, and cues based on student needs; cooperative and collaborative grouping in which students interact with a small group of diverse peers to solve a problem or reach consensus; partner interactions in which students discuss their ideas with another person; and individualized instruction in which students are provided guidance based on their unique needs. Joy Navan (2002) notes that flexible grouping benefits all students, including those with exceptionally high ability.

In high-quality English language arts instruction, teachers form student groups in at least three ways.

1. **Teacher-selected groups:** At some point during the day or week, the teacher selects which students will work in specific groups. This is most common in the guided instruction portion of the class because this is a time to focus on developing specific skills among a group of students. Because this grouping is formed out of data-specific needs at a given point in time, the group members should change regularly. The teacher makes these changes based on sound assessment information.

2. **Student-selected groups:** At other times, students select their own group members. This occurs most often with projects. Allowing students to select their group members ensures that students have complementary schedules to accomplish out-of-class learning tasks.

3. **Random groups:** Groups can also be formed randomly. This ensures that every student in the class has a chance to interact with every other student. These heterogeneous groups are used in collaborative learning when the teacher wants to ensure that the groups are mixed by ability, skills, background knowledge, fluency, and interests. Teachers can form random groups in a number of ways, including drawing names from a hat; using playing cards in which all the 3s, 4s, 5s (and so on) form groups; or counting off by numbers.

Intentional instruction, using the gradual release of responsibility model of instruction, ensures that the harmful effects of permanent ability grouping do not occur in the classroom. Importantly, flexible grouping also allows for teachers to meet with groups of students to address specific needs. Teachers should change group membership based on the assessment information. These grouping strategies ensure students will receive instruction with a variety of peers as they move through the purpose and modeling, guided instruction, productive group work, and independent learning phases of the model.

Supports for English Learners and Students With Special Needs

Instructional support targeted to specific students—like English learners and students with special needs—as part of quality core instruction is critical so students are provided with supplemental instruction or intensive intervention, as needed. If the majority of students are not provided access to high-quality instruction aligned with grade-level expectations, increasing numbers of students will need supplemental instruction, which is the focus of chapter 5 (page 75). In this chapter, we keep our attention focused on leading high-quality core instruction.

English learners and students with special needs represent important aspects of U.S. schools. Their presence in classrooms and communities is to be celebrated as part of the rich fabric of life in the United States. Unfortunately, the achievement of these students has lagged behind their peers (Fisher, Frey, & Lapp, 2012). The lack of achievement for these two groups of students has resulted in many schools and districts being labeled as failures. Instructional leaders must ensure that the instructional needs of all students are met and will likely need to assume responsibility for targeting a specific group of students for attention. The implementation of the Common Core State Standards is not going to reduce the pressure on schools to perform. To the contrary, expectations are increasing and leaders will need to redouble their efforts to ensure that all students have access to high-quality instruction.

English Learners

In the 2009–2010 school year, more than 4,700,000 English learners (10 percent of the school population) in U.S. K–12 schools received services and supports (Aud et al., 2011). These classroom supports include attention to comprehensible input and English language development methods to support language acquisition.

Comprehensible Input

Stated simply, comprehensible input is any message you can understand. For example, an English learner's comprehensible input is enhanced when the spoken message being heard is predictable and easy to understand. Using gestures and real objects (*realia*) is effective because they enhance comprehensible input, allowing the learner to use the information conveyed nonverbally to match to the spoken words. The input hypothesis ($i + 1$) is a theory of how people learn second and subsequent languages and is closely related to the theory of the *zone of proximal development* (Vygotsky, 1978). Similarly, Stephen Krashen (1985) proposes that people learn language when the message is just beyond the threshold of competence but not so difficult as to not be understood at all. For example, a second-grade teacher reads aloud the picture book *From Seed to Plant* (Gibbons, 1993) after examining seeds at several stages of development with the students. While some students may not have known vocabulary words like *seed*, *stem*, and *leaf* independently, they can now understand and use them because of the additional support of seeing the pictures and plants.

English Language Development Methods

English language development (ELD) is an overarching term used to describe a constellation of instructional approaches to ensure that students acquire English while also learning content. In other words, teachers must ensure that they infuse language goals into every activity or lesson. There are a number of specific ELD methods, such as *language brokers*, activities in which students who speak the same language but who have different proficiencies in English work together (Herrell & Jordan, 2011). There are also a number of more generic strategies that work wonders for English learners, including interactive read-alouds, structured note taking, reciprocal teaching, word sorts, and partner reading (Fisher, Brozo, Frey, & Ivey, 2011).

The English language arts classroom is an excellent place for English learners to develop both content knowledge and literacy skills. As we have noted, the gradual release of responsibility model of instruction provides time for whole-class, small-group, and independent work. This format allows the teacher to differentiate instruction and ensure that students learning English benefit from these methods. As we will discuss in greater detail in chapter 5, this model allows for supports for students not making progress to be integrated into the classroom day.

Students With Special Needs

It is likely that students with special needs—physical, cognitive, or behavioral needs—will be part of the classroom and school and thus deserve high-quality English language arts instruction. A conservative estimate indicates that there are over 6,300,000 students with special needs, representing 13.3 percent of the K–12 population (Aud et al., 2011). U.S. federal legislation, such as the Individuals With Disabilities Education Improvement Act (IDEA, 2004), requires that the students with special needs access the core academic curriculum in the general education classroom (Fisher & Frey, 2001). More important than simple compliance with federal regulations, evidence suggests that students without learning difficulties benefit academically, socially, and personally from their interactions with students with special needs (Snell & Janney, 2006).

Our experience and research suggest that students with special needs can be effectively and meaningfully educated in the general education classroom when teachers provide appropriate supports and services (Fisher, Roach, & Frey, 2002). The evidence suggests that students with special needs require access to personal, curriculum, behavioral, and technology supports (Buswell, Schaffner, & Seyler, 1999). Likely, you will have access to a special education teacher and possibly a paraprofessional to assist you in educating students with special needs in your school and classrooms (Thousand, Villa, & Nevin, 2002).

Usually, a special education support team provides accommodations and modifications to complement personal supports. Teachers may need to alter instructional materials or change an in-class activity to promote participation from students with special needs. They may also need to differentiate projects, homework, and assessments to ensure learning is meaningful. The individual education plan (IEP) team, of which the general education teacher is a member, decides to provide accommodations and modifications.

- **Accommodations:** These increase a student's access to the existing curriculum by altering how the student receives information or demonstrates mastery. Accommodations do not significantly alter what students learn, only *how* they learn it. For example, accommodations in the English language arts classroom include audio books, enlarged print, or extended time to complete an assignment.

- **Modifications:** These represent more significant changes to the curriculum itself. Most commonly, the student is responsible for mastering specific aspects of the curriculum, which reduces its difficulty. For example, a modification on a test might reduce the number of answer choices from five to three, and a modification on an essay might allow for a written outline and a spoken version.

Because accommodations and modifications cannot be evaluated out of the context in which they are being used, it is left to the IEP team to determine when the amount of changes is significant enough to constitute a modified curriculum. In that light, we have provided a list of accommodations and modifications that can be applied in the language arts classroom in table 3.2 (page 52).

With these types of supports, the English language arts classroom is a superior place for students with special needs to learn to read and write. As Paula Kluth and Julie Darmody-Latham (2003) note, the general education classroom with its focus on quality literacy instruction is an appropriate, an appealing, and a challenging place for students with special needs to learn. Diane Lea Ryndak, Andrea Morrison, and Lynne Sommerstein (1999) clearly demonstrate the benefits of providing both quality inclusive education and quality literacy instruction to students with special needs.

In every English language arts classroom, there are students with diverse learning needs, including ELs and students with special needs. We want all students to feel welcome and respected in school. This requires a concerted effort on the part of the teacher to create a sense of community in the classroom. Students need to be grouped for various instructional purposes, but making those grouping decisions can be challenging without a system for making such decisions. With all students in mind, instructional leaders must ensure that effective English language arts programs, based on high-quality instruction, are implemented on a daily basis.

Effective ELA Programs

The indicators for effective English language arts programs are not narrow and prescriptive, but rather can be accomplished using a number of different scheduling structures. As noted in the following list, the emphasis should be on sustained periods of instruction, including time each day when students read and write. The components of a quality English language arts program are the following (U.S. Department of Education, 2003).

- Every teacher is excited about reading and promotes the value and fun of reading to students.

- All students are carefully evaluated beginning in kindergarten to see what they know and what they need to do to become good readers.

- Reading instruction and practice last sixty minutes a day in kindergarten and ninety minutes or more a day in first, second, and third grade.

- All students in first, second, and third grade who are behind in reading get differentiated instruction and practice. These students receive, throughout the day, a total of sixty extra minutes of instruction when their peers are working collaboratively or independently.

Table 3.2: Teacher Accommodations and Modifications

Ideas for Use With Instructional Materials	Ideas for Use With In-Class Activities
• Tape the focus lessons. • Allow film or video supplements or in place of text. • Offer a personal dry-erase board. • Use a print enlarger or light box to illuminate text. • Use adapted computer hardware or software. • Instruct students to dictate to a partner who then writes out or types what is said. • Organize pictures instead of words into categories. • Provide visual aids to stimulate ideas for writing. • Allow the use of computers for writing. • Tape the assignment to the desk. • Provide a clipboard that can be clamped to the desk or wheelchair tray to secure papers. • Use materials on the student's reading level. • Use complementary software or adapted computer hardware.	• Break down new skills into small steps. • Underline or highlight important words and phrases. • Pick key words from the book to read on each page. • Turn pages in the book while others read. • Rewrite text or use easy-to-read versions. • Have students complete sentences orally or in writing. • Assign a peer buddy for activities. • Engage students in read, write, pair, and share activities.
Ideas for Use With Projects and Homework	**Ideas for Use With Assessments**
• Assign smaller quantities of work. • Allow more time for completion. • Encourage oral contributions. • Provide concept maps. • Provide sample sentences for students to use as a model. • Assign homework partners. • Substitute projects for written assignments.	• Underline or highlight text directions. • Reduce the number of questions by selecting representative items. • Permit oral responses to tests using a tape recorder. • Put choices for answers on index cards. • Use the sentence or paragraph as a unit of composition rather than an essay. • Use photographs in oral presentations to the class. • Reword test questions in student-friendly terms.

Visit **go.solution-tree.com/commoncore** for a reproducible version of this table.

- Classes offer before- or after-school help to all students beyond first grade who need extra instruction or who need to review skills. Summer school is available for students who are behind at the end of the year.

- Reading instruction and practice include work on letters, sounds, and blending sounds. Students learn to blend letters and sounds to form new words.

- Learning new words and their meanings is an important part of instruction.

- Students have daily spelling practice and weekly spelling tests.

- Teachers connect reading and writing on a daily basis. Students write daily, and teachers correct and return papers to the students. By the end of second grade, students write final copies of corrected papers. Teachers send papers home for parents to see.

- All students have a chance to read both silently and aloud in school each day and at home every night.

- Every classroom has a library of books that students find interesting. This includes easy books and challenging books.

- Classes visit the school library often, and it has many books. Students may check books out during the summer and over holidays.

Additionally, effective ELA programs utilize assessments for the purpose of informing instructional decisions. In addition, teachers teach skills and strategies at the letter, word, and text level and accomplish this through connections between reading and writing. Therefore, evidence-based instruction in an effective literacy program must drive the implementation of the Common Core State Standards. The following components of effective programs should be embedded into every English language arts classroom.

- **Assessment occurs throughout the academic year, and the results are used to inform instruction:** Time each week is set aside to assess student literacy progress, and collaborative teams are provided time to review the data and discuss next-steps instruction.

- **A meaningful amount of time is dedicated to literacy instruction:** Quality English language arts instruction requires class length of several hours per day at the elementary level and at least an hour per day in middle and high schools. When students struggle to maintain progress, additional time devoted to reading and writing instruction must be added, regardless of grade level.

- **Instruction is balanced between part-to-whole and whole-to-part approaches:** English language arts instruction features instruction in letters and words, reading connected text, purposeful writing, and oral language development.

- **There is a reading-writing connection:** Development of reading and writing proficiency occurs when students have rich reading experiences and opportunities for purposeful writing. As noted in the CCSS, there is a connection between reading, writing, speaking and listening, and language. Each lesson addresses several of the standards simultaneously.

- **Reading and writing occur daily:** In high-quality English language arts classrooms, these events occur with the teacher, with peers, and independently on a daily basis. No day goes by in which students fail to read and write.

The implementation of high-quality English language arts instruction is meant to form the basis for a meaningful literacy program. Within every classroom, students participate in a model of instruction that allows them to use literacy skills and strategies on a daily basis. In addition, students read and write every day, collaborate with peers, and work independently. The teacher meets with students as a whole group, in small groups, and individually. While not every student meets with the teacher every day, these meetings occur several times a week. A sample hour of instruction is provided in figure 3.2. This model will need to be modified based on the number of minutes of instruction available.

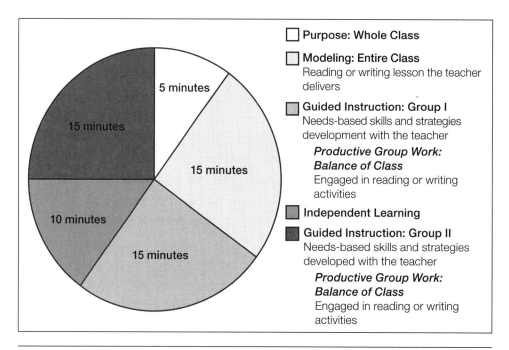

Figure 3.2: Distribution of time.

At the elementary level, English language arts instruction is typically two or three hours, which allows for additional groups of students to receive guided instruction. At the secondary level, classes may be forty-eight or fifty-five minutes, which means that each aspect must be completed more quickly. Regardless of the amount of time available, there must be a significant amount of time devoted to students actually reading and writing in the presence of their peers. This scheduling also allows the teacher to meet with small groups of students to address needs, whether those are skill deficits, language development, or extending learning.

Understanding the components of quality instruction, focusing on the right content for the right grade level, and addressing the necessary features of English language arts learning are important aspects of instructional leadership. As we noted in chapter 1, collaborative planning teams engage in discussions about what students should learn, how to assess that learning, and what to do when students do or do not learn. As we will discuss in chapter 4, accessing hard and soft data is important so leaders ensure the PLC is a whole-school or whole-district effort. In chapter 5, we will turn our focus to the importance of regularly observing classrooms so midcourse corrections can be made, including those that support English learners and students with special needs.

Conclusion

Leaders hoping to guide the implementation of the Common Core State Standards must first understand the content that teachers are expected to teach and that students are expected to learn. They must also reach agreements with teachers and staff members about high-quality instruction. Agreeing on indicators of success ensures that feedback is understood, valued, and actionable; that is, teachers can take action based on the feedback they receive. As we have noted, shared understandings and agreements are critical aspects of a leader's job responsibility. Unfortunately, it's a responsibility that is often overlooked. Instead, leaders provide feedback, and nothing changes mainly because of a lack of understanding and agreement. It's not that teachers are refusing to improve their practices, but rather, they do not agree with or understand the leader's definition of high-quality instruction. It may also be that the leader does not understand the essential components of high-quality instruction and that teachers know more. Conversations about quality open opportunities for the kind of mutual influence characteristic of shared instructional leadership, as described in chapter 1. Mutual agreements about high-quality instruction, as understood through the lens of the Common Core State Standards, increase teachers' commitment, involvement, and willingness to innovate. With these agreements in place, leaders can use a variety of tools and approaches to create change.

CHAPTER 4

Leading Change Through Data Decision Making

KEY QUESTIONS

- Think back on your experience using data to make decisions about instruction and instructional practice. What aspects of that experience will be helpful as you work with your teachers to implement the Common Core State Standards for English language arts?

- How experienced are your teachers in using data to shape their instruction? What kinds of data do they use? To what extent do they share data with one another—within and across grade levels or courses?

- How would you characterize the use of data currently in your school and district? What do you anticipate will be the impact of the CCSS on assessment practices in your school and district?

Perhaps no element of school leadership has changed more than the role of data in decision making. Gone are the days when instinct and experience alone were enough; administrators at the school and district levels are expected to be adept at collecting, analyzing, and interpreting data. Leaders design and evaluate programs based on the data they yield, and they test innovations and new programs according to their ability to influence student and teacher performance. Further, teachers, parents, and community members anticipate that data will accompany explanations of programmatic, personnel, and fiscal decisions.

To be sure, data surround us; thanks especially to achievement test scores and benchmark assessments that have come to dominate educational discourse. With the enactment of the Common Core State Standards will come a corresponding wave of new assessments. These assessments should be linked to the daily practice of gauging student understanding. In order to be what Rick Stiggins (2001) calls *assessment literate*, teachers need to "choose and develop proper methods; administer, score and interpret results; connect assessment results to specific decisions; assign grades appropriately; and communicate effectively about student achievement" (p. 11).

Data provide the fuel collaborative planning teams need to plan and improve instruction. Four critical questions drive the process for examining and analyzing this information to improve student learning, effective instruction, responsive curriculum development, and timely interventions (DuFour et al., 2008).

1. What do we want our students to learn?

2. How will we know when they have learned it?

3. How will we respond when some students don't learn?

4. How will we extend and enrich the learning for students who are already proficient?

Collaborative planning teams rely on timely access to information. But even timely data are inadequate if teams lack the time or environment conducive for completing their work. In other words, simply standing at the photocopier cranking out thick packets of charts and graphs will not automatically result in data-driven decisions. Schools thrive when accessible data, coupled with sufficient time for analysis, discussion, and action, nurture a culture of inquiry. In this context, data are useful, but without time and space to collaborate, data charts will find their way to the back of the filing cabinet as more immediate concerns overshadow them. School leaders create cultures of inquiry as they supply the fuel, and the time, for productive collaborative planning to occur. As stated in chapter 1, time *is* the essence.

Another potential pitfall comes with overlooking the data right in front of us. The results of standards assessments comprise just one source of data. Attendance data, classroom formative assessments, and student survey results further illuminate the picture that the data can paint. They give nuance and shading to enhance the bold outlines of annual test data. In this chapter, we will examine the evolving role of assessments to coincide with CCSS implementation and discuss various sources of academic and nonacademic data. Next, we will discuss ways in which data can be used to tell a coherent story and follow with tips for using the data as fuel for collaborative planning teams.

Common Core Measures of Achievement

As noted in chapter 2 (page 20), with the adoption of the Common Core has come the parallel work of designing a collaborative assessment system that can measure student progress. PARCC and SBAC were awarded over $330 million in Race to the Top funds to develop benchmark, interim, and summative assessments in English language arts and mathematics for grades 3 through 12. In addition, the Dynamic Learning Maps Alternate Assessment System Consortium (DLM) and the National Center and State Collaborative Partnership (NCSC) are developing alternate assessments for students with significant cognitive impairments, an estimated 1 percent of the U.S. school population (Aud et al., 2011). Also, the Assessment Services Supporting ELs Through Technology Systems (ASSETS) consortium is developing formative and summative assessments for use with students who are identified as ELs. The ASSETS assessments are not meant to replace those used with all students, but rather to offer a fuller picture of what each student has learned and can do. There are three major dimensions to the assessments these consortia will establish that will collectively change how we collect and analyze the data: (1) growth versus proficiency, (2) timely formative assessments, and (3) technology. (Visit www.parcconline.org, www.smarterbalanced.org, http://dynamiclearningmaps .org, and http://assets.wceruw.org for more information.)

Growth Versus Proficiency

The 2001 No Child Left Behind Act calls for increased attention to reading instruction but has yielded only marginal results. Jaekyung Lee and Todd Reeves's (2012) longitudinal analysis of achievement data from 1990 to 2009 reports that "a comparison of pre- and post-NCLB reading outcome trends showed that the level of state average achievement as well as the pace of achievement gains have either remained the same or declined after NCLB" (p. 223). One possible explanation for this may be that the data-reporting system itself has limited application. The primary data-reporting system emphasizes adequate yearly progress (AYP) and features a progressive series of cut points (annual measurable objectives, or AMOs) that accelerated rapidly after NCLB legislation went into effect. Thus, a school's progress is gauged according to its ability to meet or exceed a given year's threshold. However, these annual changes mean that schools are continually trying to hit a moving target and obscure whether growth, rather than simply proficiency, is being achieved. The resultant reports make it difficult for schools and districts to determine what is working and where additional resources should be allocated. A longstanding criticism of states' assessment systems targets their propensity to measure proficiency—status, not growth (FairTest Examiner, 2008).

In addition, most state-accountability measures describe student progress in a few broad categories (for example, California uses the terms *Far Below Basic*, *Below Basic*, *Basic*, *Proficient*, and *Advanced*), which necessarily covers a wide range of performance even within one category, making it difficult to determine the magnitude of growth from one year to another (Bettebenner & Linn, 2010). Bettebenner and Linn (2010) further explain:

> Achievement in any given year may fall short of the AMO because the school is ineffective. There are, however, a host of other reasons besides ineffective instruction that can lead to low achievement. The students may have had low achievement in previous years and despite substantial growth in the year in question, may still fall short of the AMO. A school that makes AYP may have students who started the year with relatively high achievement as the result of favorable home conditions and support whereas a school that fails to make AYP may do so because its students start the year with low achievement as the result of unfavorable family conditions and educational support in prior years. (p. 15)

The new assessment systems promise to yield growth information as well as proficiency status. This depends on the development of vertical scales that will allow for reliable measures of student growth across grade levels. (Because existing state standards are generally not organized as a progression, there has been noticeable variability in difficulty from one grade level to the next.) In addition, measures of progress toward college- and career-ready goals will be included. This means that at least three data reports (growth information, proficiency status, and progress toward CCR) will be available for each student. Both PARCC and SBAC will provide more information about student performance that will allow for more accurate measures of individual student growth and can include data on the optional formative assessments administered at the beginning and middle of the school year.

Timely Formative Assessments

Importantly, the five consortia's assessments will feature optional interim data for gauging student progress within two weeks of test administration. These data will not be used for accountability purposes, as this will be reserved for the summative end-of-year assessments only. Formative assessments should allow collaborative teams to make mid-course corrections and design interventions to meet the needs of students before the summative assessments. These formative assessment data reports will be linked to an array of support materials, including a digital library of resources, online professional development modules, and classroom practice tasks.

Technology

Technology is the third dimension of the assessments that will change. Computer adaptive testing (CAT) is a feature of both PARCC and SBAC assessments. The computer program used in the assessments adjusts the difficulty of questions based on student responses. This process is particularly beneficial for students with special needs and those who struggle with learning. These modified assessments will provide teachers with a more detailed picture of student performance, enabling them to differentiate instruction.

In most grades, students are likely to be assessed on computers rather than paper. Computerized assessments are efficient: results can be delivered in weeks, not months. Faster access to results, particularly those on interim assessments, means that teachers can more readily adjust instruction to meet the needs of their students. Furthermore, computerized assessments provide for a variety of item questions and response styles, uses of technology, and student interactivity. The consortia are developing prototype items that educators can review (see www.smarterbalanced.org and www.parcconline.org for more information about the prototypes and technology requirements).

A significant number of the standards call for mastery of research using digital resources, analyses of video and audio sources, and use of multimedia. For example, the standards suggest that students who are college and career ready "use technology and digital media strategically and capably" (NGA & CCSSO, 2010a, p. 7). Therefore, the assessments will need to mirror the instructional tools and curricula utilized in the classroom. To be sure, this will pose a considerable challenge to schools in terms of infrastructure, data management, and student access. A number of outstanding questions revolve around using the Internet with younger students, as well as around security issues. However, there is no question that electronic test taking will continue to persevere and provide any number of innovative techniques that will enhance the validity of the tests. For example, teachers can use new technologies to enhance the use of Universal Design for Learning (UDL) principles, such that they provide multiple means of representation, action and expression, and engagement (for more information, visit www.udlcenter.org). In addition, teachers can make useful accommodations for students with special needs, such as using an American Sign Language (ASL) avatar for students who use sign language. Furthermore, teachers can use online simulations to test English learners, allowing for separation of content knowledge from language proficiency (www.primarygames.com/arcade/simulation.php). Questions remain about how teachers will test collaborative skills, an identified 21st century skill, but once again, technology is likely to play a key role.

The Language of Data

Thus far we have only described quantitative achievement data, but any educator will tell you that this offers a limited portrait of a student. In addition to the quantitative data, or *hard* data, there is also qualitative, or *soft* data. When examined together in a thoughtful way, hard and soft data illuminate both what and how a student learns. School leaders are wise to make both hard and soft data available to collaborative teams so they can determine what is effective and where they can make instructional improvements. In order to do so, leaders must be familiar with the language of assessment. Whether using quantitative or qualitative data, educators must make the purpose for the assessment clear.

Purposes for Assessment

Watching the work of the various consortia as they move through the process of developing Common Core State Standards assessments has been fascinating. While the uninitiated might wonder why it seems so protracted, in truth, the process requires careful consideration of technical measurements, including ensuring that issues of validity and reliability have been fully addressed. The journey to developing effective assessments begins with determining what purpose it should serve. Diane Lapp, Douglas Fisher, James Flood, and Arturo Cabello (2001) describe four such purposes. The assessment should:

1. Diagnose individual student needs (for example, assessing developmental status, monitoring and communicating student progress, certifying competency, and determining needs)

2. Inform instruction (for example, evaluating instruction, modifying instructional strategies, and identifying instructional needs)

3. Evaluate programs

4. Provide accountability information

A major challenge facing the consortia in developing the CCSS assessments is that, unlike past practice, they are charged with developing a suite of assessments. For example, the assessment map for PARCC features several different kinds of assessments for grades 3–8 and high school (see figure 4.1, page 62).

The first two assessments are formative and aimed at making future instructional decisions rather than intended for accountability and program-evaluation purposes. Additionally, PARCC suggests a flexible summative assessment to enhance instruction, not for accountability. Lastly, the plan uses two summative measures for accountability

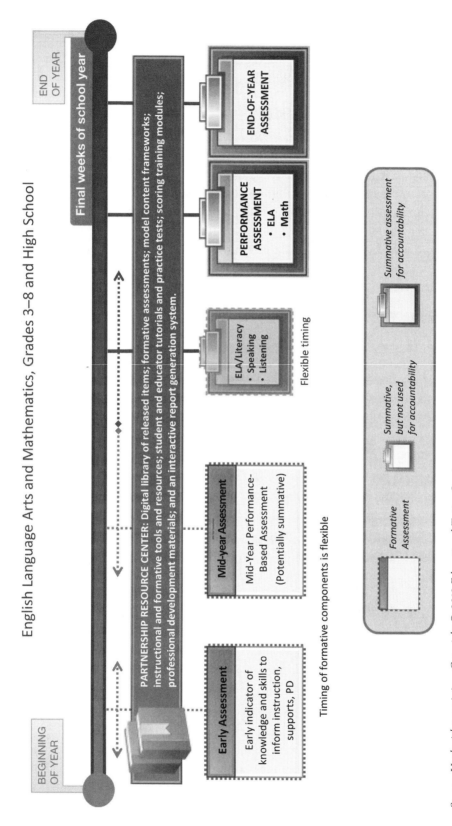

English Language Arts and Mathematics, Grades 3–8 and High School

BEGINNING OF YEAR

END OF YEAR

Final weeks of school year

Early Assessment

Early indicator of knowledge and skills to inform instruction, supports, PD

Mid-year Assessment

Mid-Year Performance-Based Assessment (Potentially summative)

Timing of formative components is flexible

PARTNERSHIP RESOURCE CENTER: Digital library of released items; formative assessments; model content frameworks; instructional and formative tools and resources; student and educator tutorials and practice tests; scoring training modules; professional development materials; and an interactive report generation system.

ELA/Literacy
• Speaking
• Listening

Flexible timing

PERFORMANCE ASSESSMENT
• ELA
• Math

END-OF-YEAR ASSESSMENT

Formative Assessment

Summative, but not used for accountability

Summative assessment for accountability

Source: Used with permission. Copyright © 2013 Educational Testing Service. www.ets.org

Figure 4.1: PARCC comprehensive assessment plan.

and program evaluation (Center for K–12 Assessment and Performance Management, 2012). The five types of assessment are the following.

1. **Formative (diagnostic early assessment):** An assessment at the beginning of the year for diagnosis and planning

2. **Formative (midyear assessment):** A midyear assessment to evaluate performance

3. **Summative (not for accountability):** A flexibly timed assessment to measure student performance in the Speaking and Listening standards

4. **Summative (performance assessment for accountability):** A performance assessment over the ELA and mathematics standards

5. **Summative (end-of-year assessment for accountability):** An assessment in the final weeks of the school year

SBAC has a similar assessment map for grades 3–8 and high school, but it differs from PARCC in terms of timing and delivery (Center for K–12 Assessment and Performance Management, 2012). The first two formative (SBAC calls them *interim*) assessments are not used for accountability purposes, and like PARCC, they are linked to resources for teachers to use after the results are compiled (see figure 4.2, page 64). Notably, both interim assessments are computer based. In the last twelve weeks of the school year, the plan suggests teachers use two summative assessments to measure student performance and for accountability purposes; one is computer based.

- **Formative (interim):** A computer-based assessment at the beginning of the school year for planning

- **Formative (interim):** A second computer-based assessment at midyear for planning

- **Summative (performance task):** Performance tasks in ELA, writing, and mathematics used for accountability

- **Summative:** A computer-based assessment used for accountability that includes a retake option

The suite of assessments these consortia are developing will offer teachers and administrators a broader range of data to analyze. However, these new assessments pose a challenge. Most teachers have become familiar with reading and interpreting current state testing results and rarely look at these with an eye toward formative assessment. In fact, most of us have accepted that the long delay in reporting makes any kind of responsive planning impossible. After all, test results that don't arrive until summer mean that one's own students have moved on to the next grade level. These new assessments, which will be administered beginning in the fall of 2014, comprise diagnostic, formative, summative, and accountability purposes. It will be imperative that teachers understand what data they are analyzing and what they should do with the results. Until the 2014–15 school year, school leaders are wise to orient teachers to their state's assessment map,

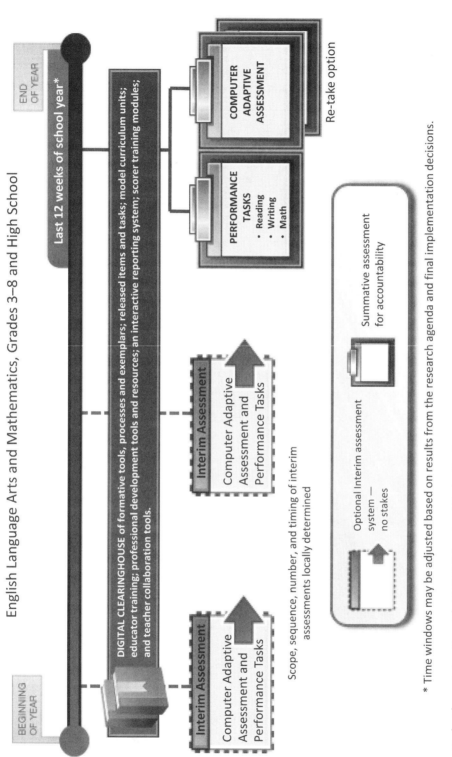

Source: Used with permission. Copyright © 2013 Educational Testing Service. www.ets.org

Figure 4.2: SBAC comprehensive assessment plan.

providing targeted professional development on the purposes for various assessment and how the results of each should be applied. Leaders and teachers can also develop their own questions based on the standards themselves to determine students' understanding. Consistent with the PLC at Work model, these common formative assessments should provide collaborative planning teams with information about student achievement and performance aligned with the Common Core State Standards.

But, large-scale standards tests are not the only data collaborative planning teams can and should examine. Teachers' own classroom practice can yield relevant and timely data that collaborative teams can analyze to make instructional decisions. High-quality classroom data depend on whether opportunities for harvesting data are thoughtfully planned or simply neglected. After all, it is easy for us to slip into a pattern of not collecting data because we are simply too busy. The irony is that collecting and analyzing classroom data can actually save time because the resulting instruction becomes more focused. How can this be accomplished? By making sure that teachers are *assessment literate*.

Hard Data

Hard data, simply put, are numbers that describe. More specifically, they answer the questions *who*, *what*, and *when*. For example, we use these hard data to describe: 46 percent of seventh-grade English students scored at the proficient or advanced levels on the winter 2015 interim assessment in the area of vocabulary. Of course, hard data are not limited to large-scale assessments; we also describe classroom-based assessments in this manner: 27 percent of the third-period seventh-grade English class could identify five examples of the author's use of figurative language in today's close-reading lesson (for example, see RL.7.4). These data have some use in that they describe, but they become more compelling when used for *comparative purposes*: 27 percent of the third-period seventh-grade English class could identify five examples of the author's use of figurative language in today's close-reading lesson. However, 58 percent of the fourth-period class was able to do the task. This comparative use now begs a question: Why? That comparative question is what drives data analysis. A collaborative planning team of seventh-grade English teachers can use this comparative question to query its instructional practice. What were the contributing factors that resulted in fourth period's stronger performance? These hard data also inform the development of better formative assessments. For example, the collaborative planning team may speculate on how the hard data were collected. Was it a multiple-choice quiz or free response? The team might also examine at what point during the close-reading lesson the teacher collected these data. Most importantly, these hard data can be the catalyst for deepening shared knowledge as the team discusses the appropriateness of teaching objectives, the extent to which students knew the lesson's purpose, and whether further instruction is warranted.

Soft Data

When paired with soft data, hard data are further contextualized. *Soft data* is a term used to describe the qualitative information that numbers cannot adequately convey. Rather, these data are represented through words. An examination of the soft data in the seventh-grade English classrooms can reveal the extent to which students applied their knowledge of figurative language in an end-of-period written explanation of the author's purpose for using figurative language (for example, see RL.7.5). The analysis that follows requires that the teacher make a qualitative assessment of the student's use of evidence to support claims.

Collection is critical in understanding soft data. In large part, they are gathered through observation and conversation. Written student work is one source for gleaning soft data, which has an advantage of being a permanent product that teams can refer to later. However, much of the qualitative information is found through listening and watching. For instance, grouping the kinds and characteristics of the types of questions students ask during the close-reading lesson can help us further understand the hard data. A qualitative analysis of the classroom discourse in periods three and four might reveal that the teacher's questions in the earlier period were lower level and mostly procedural in nature, while those in the next period had a higher rate of questions that probed analysis and evaluation skills. These soft data could come from colleagues' observations or from the individual teacher recording the discourse in both periods for this purpose. The collaborative planning team's subsequent conversation might include queries about differences in student background knowledge in the two periods and even frank discussion about expectations for each group.

Formative Uses of Hard and Soft Data

Perhaps the most critical work that a collaborative planning team engages in when examining data concerns *how* to use them. If the primary outcome is simply to examine what has occurred in the past, then it is unlikely that any substantial change will ever occur. Reeves (2005) likens this to an autopsy, where the only resultant information is in identifying the cause of death. However, he states that interim assessments are comparable to checkups in that they yield information about present conditions and prescribed changes in behavior or medication that are designed to prevent future problems. Note that we have intentionally not equated summative data with autopsies and formative data with checkups. We have seen both kinds of assessments used for both of these purposes. Summative data can and should result in future actions. A fourth-grade collaborative planning team that examines the achievement scores of last year's third-grade students can plan for instruction and intervention efforts even before their students arrive for the new school year. Formative data can be underutilized as well. If these interim assessments do not trigger teacher action, they essentially become an endless series of casual autopsies.

Whether teachers consider formative or summative assessments, and hard or soft data, a collaborative planning team's effectiveness is directly tied to its commitment to regularly collect and analyze assessment data. While the most apparent source is hard data from Common Core State Standards' achievement results, teams must understand their analyses are not limited to these data sources. As a school leader, you can instruct teams to create a schedule for collecting both hard and soft data via formative and summative assessments that they can use each time they meet.

For example, a collaborative planning team consisting of third-, fourth-, and fifth-grade teachers develops a calendar of data activities for the first quarter of the school year (see table 4.1).

Table 4.1: Sample Data Collection and Analysis Calendar

Date	Source	Type	Purpose	Method for Collection	Team Analysis Date
Aug. 13–17	Last year's test scores	Hard data: Summative	Intervention	District, school, and student reports	**Aug. 17**
Aug. 20–24	District ELA readiness assessment	Hard and soft data: Formative	Diagnostic	Interviews and group administration	**Aug. 29**
Sept. 10–14	Informal reading inventories	Soft data: Formative	Instructional and grouping	Individual students and their teachers one on one	**Sept. 19**
Oct. 1–5	Student writing samples	Hard and soft data: Summative	Consensus scoring protocol	Group administration	**Oct. 10**
Oct. 15–25	Peer observations	Hard and soft data: Formative	Collaborative discussions	Structured classroom walkthroughs	**Oct. 31**

Visit **go.solution-tree.com/commoncore** for a reproducible version of this table.

The teachers begin by scheduling an examination of the hard data available to them from the previous year's state standards assessments. Leaders can be involved in these conversations or can ensure that collaborative planning teams have the time to engage in these discussions.

"We schedule this for the planning week before students arrive," explains fourth-grade teacher Rachel Aquino. "It's so easy to get swept up in all the preparation and forget to spend time learning about the students who will be new to us."

Ms. Aquino and her colleague, third-grade teacher Scott Thomas, serve as the liaisons for collecting the district, school, and student reports. Mr. Thomas says, "This gives us a very good idea of who is going to benefit from in-class and after-school intervention efforts beginning the first day. There's no reason to wait until the end of the quarter to start the conversation about who needs help. We *know* who needs help. It's up to us to act on it."

The team also marks the first week of school with students as a time to gather the kinds of hard and soft data that the district English language arts assessment yields. Ms. Aquino notes, "This used to be a district benchmark assessment, before the new assessment suites were developed. We've repurposed portions of it to give us some 'quick and dirty' information about how students are doing currently."

Mr. Thomas agrees. "There's a great section on editing sentences, and another multiple choice section on vocabulary knowledge," he says. "But I think the part I like most is the interview protocol for asking students about their interests and reading habits."

The teachers use these brief assessments when they meet the following week to discuss their findings and to make grouping decisions. "Most of it confirms what last year's data revealed, but sometimes there's a surprise," says Ms. Aquino. "I found two students in my class who did poorly on last year's assessment, and when I interviewed them I learned about their lack of motivation for reading. I talked with the team, and now I have some different ideas about how to reach them."

During the remainder of the first quarter, the team analyzes the informal reading inventories to make grouping decisions and a consensus scoring date for collaboratively analyzing student work. "We have two new members of our team this year," says Mr. Thomas, "and both are coming from primary school. We realized that making sure we have some consensus scoring throughout the year will assist us in discussing shared expectations about student learning."

The team plans on finishing the first quarter with a series of structured learning walks through each other's classrooms. Ms. Aquino says, "Our principal hires a team of roving subs each quarter so we can walk through each other's classrooms. This is probably the most valuable thing we do, because it allows us to see what happens within our grade level, and across the grade-level band." She shakes her head back and forth as she says, "It's hard to imagine we didn't used to do this. I understand so much more about fourth grade, because I witness the learning and instruction that occur in third and fifth grades."

Valuable Data Sources

While the majority of this chapter concerns achievement data, we would be remiss to overlook the nonachievement data, especially less common sources of information. At the top of our list is attendance data. These are readily available hard data, made infinitely simpler to gather and analyze using the electronic student management systems common in schools. However, in too many schools, the only people who see the attendance data reports are administrators, counselors, and clerks. Teachers might look at their own class attendance data, but they rarely get an opportunity to see larger data sets. Small data sets don't allow for seeing patterns and observing trends.

As an example, consider a career-focused high school. This high school offers an extensive internship program. Each week, students in grades 9–12 spend a full day at a health-related internship site. The majority of these placements are at local hospitals, and teachers see the direct positive effects of these experiences on students in their technical reading and writing skills, vocabulary knowledge, and communication expertise. Still, students don't recognize these benefits if they miss school on their internship days. One collaborative planning team at the school discovers that there are students who are habitually absent on internship days. By identifying these students, leaders and teachers were able to intervene directly. In some cases absenteeism was due to dissatisfaction with the particular placement. The internship coordinator easily rectifies these situations, moving chronically absent students to different parts of the hospital. One student confesses that her scrubs are too small, and she was too embarrassed to request a nonstandard larger size so she simply stays home. This same team also looks at the correspondence between tardies and internship days. Individual meetings with these students reveal that many of them deliberately arrive after the internship bus leaves the school so they can catch up on late assignments and study for upcoming tests. Teachers make plans and contracts with each of these students so he or she can receive additional help without sacrificing internship experiences.

As a school leader, you have a responsibility to provide collaborative planning teams with the data they need to analyze learning progress in light of the whole student. Nonachievement data, such as attendance rates, provide another dimension beyond academic performance levels on an examination of English language arts content. Importantly, these data further illuminate the needs and strengths of individual students who struggle despite our efforts. To be sure, students may be challenged with concerns related to transportation, nutrition, and family involvement that are not wholly the responsibility of the classroom teacher. However, teachers almost unfailingly know when a student of theirs is in trouble. A collaborative planning team offers additional eyes and ears for exploring a potential problem. To do the job, the team needs data, both hard and soft. Using a thoughtful process for spotlighting struggling students is a necessary first step for marshaling the school's resources for intervening.

A Coherent Data Story

Data driven can quickly devolve into *data overload* if there is no effort to tell a coherent story about a school, grade level, or individual student. A fragmented approach to examining the data will result in a splintered picture, like looking at one's reflection in a badly cracked mirror. Collaborative planning teams within a school that is engaged in a PLC process provide ideal vehicles for ensuring that a coherent picture emerges. However, the teams need a structure for examining and reporting on data in a way that ensures that evidence supports all decisions. As noted previously, DuFour et al. (2008) advise using four guiding questions concerning student learning (see page 2). These questions can be adapted to discuss data usage.

1. What will data tell us about our expectations for student learning?

2. How will we use data so we know when students have learned the content?

3. What data are necessary for us to have so we can respond when some students don't learn?

4. What data will help us identify students who are already proficient so that we can extend and enrich their learning?

Taken together, these data questions provide collaborative planning teams with a way of understanding their own students and the professional learning community at large.

What Will Data Tell Us About Our Expectations for Student Learning?

This first question focuses on teachers' instructional practice. There is a wealth of hard and soft data just waiting to be gathered through structured walks of classrooms. The ways that we interact with our students and the curriculum speak volumes about our expectations for their success. These translate to the expectations we hold for our students. Daniel Sciarra and Katherine Ambrosino (2011) utilize high school expectations data from over 5,000 students, teachers, and parents who participated in the Educational Longitudinal Study from 2002 to 2006. The researchers followed students for two years after high school graduation to determine postsecondary outcomes. The results indicate that teacher expectations of whether students would pursue a two- or four-year degree after high school are the strongest predictor of enrollment and continuation. The implications for school leaders, according to the researchers, are clear: "Help teachers . . . understand the predictive consequences of their expectations for their students and emphasize the importance of elevating their expectations even in the face of evidence that may challenge them from doing so" (Sciarra & Ambrosino, 2011, p. 238). Given that the keystone of the Common Core State Standards is predicated on preparing students to be college and career ready, the role of teacher expectations cannot be undersold. The influence of elementary teacher expectancy on reading achievement is less clearly pronounced, but there are important exceptions. Benjamin J. Hinnant, Marion O'Brien, and Sharon Ghazarian (2009) find that teacher expectations from first through fifth grade have little effect on reading achievement for most students. However:

> Teacher expectations of children's reading abilities were related to later performance for one potentially vulnerable group of children: minority boys. Minority boys had the lowest performance when their abilities were underestimated and the greatest gains when their abilities were overestimated. (p. 669)

We communicate our expectations through the ways in which we interact with students, the amount of time we allow them to hear each other's voices, and the manner in which we use goal setting and assessment to elevate or deflate a student's sense of agency. As Hinnant et al. (2009) note, this is particularly important for minority students like ELs. These interactions are difficult to discern when one is in the moment. Structured walks, peer observations, and coaching all provide teachers with the qualitative and quantitative data they need to be reflective and continuously improve. Utilize your influence as a school leader to provide the necessary time and resources for teams to accomplish this important work. This may involve providing substitutes to cover classes, creative use of planning and preparation time, and even shifting the focus from traditional professional development to experiences that foster collegial conversations as discussed in chapter 1.

How Will We Use Data So We Know When Students Have Learned the Content?

Two words answer this question: *formative assessment*. First, without a means to collect and analyze student formative assessment data, opportunities for reteaching are squandered. Second, a collaborative planning team fails its own mission—to collaboratively plan—when it fails to act on the data it has collected. The role of the school leader is clear in this regard: communicating clear expectations for data use with collaborative planning teams. Team members also need the necessary skills to collect, understand, and analyze formative assessment data. A collaborative planning team that lacks such skills should receive the necessary training and resources so members are able to utilize data to inform future instruction.

What Data Are Necessary for Us to Have So We Can Respond When Some Students Don't Learn?

A collaborative planning team thrives when it has access to meaningful data. We have known some school leaders who are reluctant to share all available data with teachers, and we have never understood why. If teams are to make data-driven decisions, they need the complete picture. At our school, we share *unfiltered* standardized achievement data with teachers. Filtered data remove the scores of students who don't meet reporting parameters, such as being enrolled for less than a prescribed period. These filtering mechanisms are necessary for public reporting purposes, and they are designed to preserve testing fidelity for accountability purposes. However, the students who attend our school are real, and filtering their results means that we aren't paying close attention to all our students.

Another valuable source of information that is frequently withheld from teachers is cluster data (subtests) that further narrow standardized data reports. For instance, teams benefit tremendously when they know that last year's students performed well on vocabulary tasks but had significantly lower achievement in the area of furnishing evidence in their writing. These cluster data should be shared in order for teams to focus their efforts. Finally, some school leaders do not share data because they assume the data will be of little assistance. Consider how a K–2 team uses library circulation data to support students.

"Our media specialist runs monthly reports on book circulation and time devoted to digital resources in the school library," says first-grade teacher Beth Oppenheimer. "What's interesting is that the reports include after-school time as well. Now each teacher on our team has identified students in our classrooms who warrant more attention, especially more time devoted to reading." She continues, "This year, we have a new principal who started sharing the media specialist's reports with us. Our team had never seen them before. In fact, we didn't even know there was such a thing. But it got us thinking. We all had students who needed more time reading print and digital sources, but we had only counted what happened right in front of us. We forgot that there are many more opportunities throughout the day."

Ms. Oppenheimer's collaborative planning team began tracking students identified as being at risk using the monthly media specialist reports. Many of them also attended the school's after-school program. "We got additional staff involved in targeting these students," Ms. Oppenheimer says. "When students came in the library, the media specialist greeted them and had a book or other resource set aside for them. 'I was thinking of you and how much you like soccer, so I set aside this book for you,' she would say to a student. The after-school staff joined in as well. They made sure that these students were using their time productively on the computers and tablets in the library. We began to see gains in book circulation and logged Internet time on these reports," says Ms. Oppenheimer. "We could also track the pages students were on and how many minutes they spent on each page. We have gained so much insight into what these students are doing with their time, and it's helping us teach the organizational, stamina, and persistence skills they need to stick with reading."

Without access to data, leaders and collaborative planning teams cannot respond and ensure that students have access to high-quality instruction and intervention. Failure to collect and analyze student performance data means that the school is not operating as a PLC because in a PLC, data drive the system. Teams that meet to simply talk about what they like to do or how they like to teach are not likely to have the profound impact on student learning expected of the PLC at Work process.

What Data Will Help Us Identify Students Who Are Already Proficient So That We Can Extend and Enrich Their Learning?

The same kinds of practices discussed in regard to the previous three questions should be applied to students who are working above grade-level expectations. Too often in our understandable efforts to address the needs of students who struggle, we overlook those who are doing quite well. Remind teachers about this population. First, teacher expectations about high-achieving students can have a positive or negative effect on student learning. Lannie Kanevsky and Tacey Keighley (2003) interviewed high school students identified as gifted but nonetheless underperformed. In their research, they find that boredom is often at the root of their lack of achievement and that five Cs—control, choice, challenge, complexity, and caring teachers—are the factors that influence whether or not they perform in each class (Kanevsky & Keighley, 2003). Second, formative assessments, including those teachers administer at the beginning of a unit of instruction, can identify proficient students and ensure that choices are offered to challenge these students and prevent boredom. Third, the data available on students who are performing well can be adequately tracked and discussed in collaborative planning meetings.

The eighth-grade English teachers of a collaborative planning team arrange for the students who score proficient on formative assessments to expand their learning through cross-age peer tutoring in sixth- and seventh-grade classes. Once a week, these students meet with their younger counterparts, who have also been identified as proficient on the formative assessments for their current unit of study. These students engage in discussions of short stories the team identifies for the purposes of enrichment. As these groups of students interact, the teachers can focus their attention on students who have yet to demonstrate proficiency on the formative assessments.

"This has been a great addition to our curriculum," says sixth-grade English teacher Ned Porter. "The eighth graders get the reading two weeks in advance and make a plan for the discussion," he says. "The seventh and sixth graders get it the week before, and they all meet after the reading is done to talk about it. They've read short stories by Edgar Allan Poe, O. Henry, and Isaac Asimov. The one they're reading this week is 'A Sound of Thunder' by Ray Bradbury." Mr. Porter concludes, "I think the thing I like the most is that it's not always the same kids. We see some changes from one unit to the next. I thought this would involve just a few kids, but 20 percent of the students in our classes have been in at least one short story discussion this year."

Conclusion

A school leader can ensure that collaborative planning teams are able to make the most of the hard and soft data that describe student learning. A critical first step is to make sure that teams have access to timely and complete data. In addition, teams benefit from a structure that allows them to apply the data in ways that yield decisions that make a difference. The key questions presented in this chapter are designed to advance these conversations. Finally, even the very best teams will be hampered without adequate time and resources to examine, discuss, and act on data. Providing resources that allow team members to observe each other in action is necessary for fostering the changes in curriculum and instruction that the Common Core State Standards demand.

CHAPTER 5

Leading Change Through Structures That Support Teachers and Students

KEY QUESTIONS

- How would you describe your leadership style? Which leadership practices do you follow to facilitate shared leadership with your faculty and staff?

- Which structures now in place in your school most effectively support teachers as they strive to improve student learning? What do you think will be the impact of implementing the CCSS on these structures?

- How often and for what purposes do you visit classrooms? How do you and the teachers use your observations and conversations to facilitate collaborative planning?

- To what extent and degree of success has RTI been implemented in your school? What changes do you think may be needed to strengthen supplemental instruction and intensive intervention? What resources do your teachers require to fulfill the expectations of RTI in the context of implementing the CCSS?

- How will you use collaborative planning teams to develop structures that support teachers and students?

Instructional leaders face the monumental task of maintaining current efforts during a time of great change: improving instruction, developing teachers, using data wisely, and heading intervention efforts. Without question, the work ahead will be complex. There may even be a temptation to go it alone in the belief that putting yourself in charge of all these efforts will somehow allow you to control for the errors. But nothing could be further from the truth. A foundational PLC concept is to focus on examining student learning through collective inquiry and then taking action to improve it (DuFour, DuFour, Eaker, & Many, 2006). This springs from a belief in shared leadership as the conduit for change. Consider the implications of those two words: *shared* and *leadership*. *Shared* describes the importance of the collective community in the change process. Much like a bandleader without a band, there's no music without the musicians. But *leadership* is equally essential. Without someone to make sure the musicians play the same music in unison, there is noise but no artistry. A school leader cannot devolve into a one-person band. Neither can he or she just hope that everyone will somehow agree on a piece and begin playing the same tune at the same time in the agreed-on way. An effective leader balances both sharing and leadership in order to achieve change.

The purpose of this chapter is to discuss the leadership practices necessary to foster a sense of shared leadership and maintain a focus on student learning. We will begin with a discussion of a useful framework for equipping collaborative planning teams to assess student learning in order to generate meaningful data for their conversations. The section that follows will shift to the parallel work of the school leader in providing teachers with informative feedback about teaching practices. We will follow with methods for conducting collaborative classroom visits that ensure continuous progress. Finally, we will end the chapter with advice on coordinating intervention efforts at your school.

Collaborative Curriculum Audit

With the adoption and implementation of the CCSS, a troubling realization arises: a once-aligned curriculum is no longer so. Years of careful accumulation of materials, practices, and processes may or may not correspond with new expectations of student learning. As noted in chapter 4, data are the fuel of the collaborative planning teams. But these same teams may have difficulty determining when, where, and in what ways to collect the quantitative and qualitative information they need to make decisions about these new expectations.

An excellent starting point is for grade bands (not single grade levels or courses) to conduct an informal curriculum audit. By doing so, teams can determine what they already offer, make decisions about realignment as needed, and identify gaps. This audit is a useful counter to a question likely to arise when faced with a new set of standards: *When do the new textbooks arrive?* By encouraging teams to begin with a self-audit, they may discover that they need fewer new resources than originally anticipated.

Curriculum audits can be large, formal affairs; we don't believe that these are the best tools to meet the particular purpose of leading the implementation of the Common Core State Standards. An internal audit should focus on a limited number of issues so that the audit doesn't take on a life of its own. We recommend that teams narrow their focus to four issues.

1. What instructional materials do we currently possess?

2. What instructional practices do we currently use to support students at, below, and above grade level?

3. What assessments inform us about their progress?

4. How do we respond when a student is not making progress?

Teams can gather data through a variety of methods, and they should use a mixture of them in order to paint a more complete picture. An inventory checklist or analysis of documents can help answer the first question, regarding instructional materials. Teams can address the second, concerning instructional practices, through observations of teachers' classrooms. Team members can add information to a collaborative online calendar to determine the third question, about assessments. The team can administer a survey to answer the fourth, regarding intervention responses. Once they have done so, the teams should analyze these hard and soft data in order to identify strengths and gaps and redesign curricula and pacing guides (see page 78).

While this audit represents a significant amount of work for the teams, it is necessary in order for them to move beyond unpacking the standards to taking action. The teams will benefit from a timeline for these steps to be completed. The initial work of the curriculum audit and pacing guides will probably need to occur only once. Development and consensus scoring of formative assessments will be repeated each year. Importantly, the process of revision and intervention is ongoing.

The intent of these processes is to collectively empower teachers to actively participate in the change process, rather than having change dictated to them. With changes to curricular, instructional, and assessment practices comes the attendant demands on classroom practice. School leaders should anticipate that a shift to implement the CCSS may cause anxiety and stress for even the most capable and confident teachers. Therefore, it is vital that the six practices of a PLC (see pages 1–2) are used as a means to develop teacher effectiveness and efficacy.

Feed Up, Feed Back, and Feed Forward

The impact a teacher has on student learning is of the utmost importance. To ensure that student learning outcomes occur, leaders should spend significant amounts of their time supporting the PLC process in which teachers examine evidence of student learning from their common assessments and use that evidence to inform and improve their individual and collective practice (DuFour, DuFour, Eaker, & Karhanek, 2010). As we will elaborate on in this chapter, leaders establish collaborative team meetings and provide teachers the support and training they need to engage with their colleagues. When it comes time to improve practice, common formative assessment systems can play a role. Much like taking action based on student learning, leaders can take action based on teacher learning.

John Hattie and Helen Timperley (2007) have an elegant way of describing a model of ongoing assessment for students: feed up, feed back, and feed forward. We have taken this model a step further to articulate a concrete plan for doing so, one in which we add checking for understanding to the mix (Frey & Fisher, 2011) as a way to *feed up* by using methods to analyze and assess student understanding. Additionally, we offer a protocol for developing common pacing guides and curricula. Consider how these principles apply when supporting teacher growth.

Feed Up by Establishing Purpose

When teachers know what is expected of learners, what students should be learning, and how students can demonstrate mastery, they accelerate learners' acquisition of knowledge. This requires clear statements of purpose in order to orient teachers and make professional learning intentional. As teachers, we are long accustomed to the practice of defining learning objectives for a lesson: "Students will analyze how an author uses and transforms source material." However, how often are these learning targets shared with the people who are supposed to demonstrate them? Even less common is the practice of stating purposes for fellow adults: "The purpose of this meeting is to analyze how writing for argumentation can be strengthened in ninth-grade English" (for example, see W.9.1). Establishing purpose means that these intentions are shared with the teams and are used as a guideline for the formative assessment that follows.

Checking for Understanding

Checking for understanding is an ongoing process of assessment to determine to what extent a teacher understands and to find out what gaps in knowledge may remain. As such, checking for understanding lies at the heart of formative assessment and is probably the first thing that comes to mind when teachers think about assessment. There are a variety of methods for checking for understanding, including oral language activities, reciprocal teaching, questions, writing, projects and performances, and tests. Leaders can use these tools to determine understanding. For example, a targeted question may reveal a misconception, or an exit slip at the end of a collaborative planning team discussion may identify a deep understanding of student performance. Checking for understanding requires careful listening and observation, especially in using this self-query: "What does this teacher know and not know that would lead him or her to utilize that practice or process?" By foregrounding this question with classroom observations and conversations with individual teachers, you can hypothesize what the teacher needs next to support his or her learning.

Developing Common Pacing Guides and Curricula

The Common Core State Standards for English language arts will present a new set of challenges for teachers and administrators. Common assessments, consensus scoring, and item analysis will figure prominently in developing new pacing guides and curricula. The five steps to developing common pacing guides and curricula include the following (Fisher & Frey, 2007).

1. Construct an initial pacing guide for instruction. Designed to frame the teams' work, this guide should be aligned to the expectations in the CCSS.

2. Identify instructional and curriculum materials such as texts, websites, and media for each unit of study in the pacing guide.

3. Develop common assessments and a schedule for administering them. These should include formative and summative measures and will provide the collaborative teams with data to analyze.

4. Engage in consensus scoring and item analysis. These actions serve to determine how students did and to explore the relationship between teaching and learning. It is useful to disaggregate the data to identify trends within and across significant subpopulations. The intent is not to drill down to the individual teacher level, but rather to look across the grade level and grade band

to locate patterns and to drill down to individual student performance levels so that interventions can be developed. For example, if students with special needs are making good progress, then what accommodations can this be attributed to? Remember that these data-analysis events are also for identifying areas of instructional strength, not just locating areas of need.

5. Make revisions to instruction and curriculum, and form intervention groups. The outcomes of these meetings should have dual purposes. The first is to refine instruction for all students in order to improve acquisition of knowledge. In addition, the team needs to examine the circumstances that might be preventing identified students from making sufficient progress. For some students, this may be a matter of reteaching. Those who are displaying a pattern of difficulties may warrant more formal intervention. Later in this chapter, we will discuss RTI as a model for meeting the needs of students who struggle.

Feed Back to Build Teacher Agency

It would be a mistake to isolate checking for understanding from the feedback loop. All learners need feedback to guide their learning. This is true for kindergarten students learning their letters as well as teachers learning about assessment data. Leaders are expected to provide feedback to teachers about their work. But not all feedback is useful. In fact, sometimes feedback makes the person receiving it defensive. Consider the following forms of feedback.

*   **Feedback about the task (corrective feedback)** is effective for alerting someone to errors but can be ineffective if the person does not know what to do to correct the error. For example, providing a teacher with feedback about specific assessment items and the ways in which the items can diagnose errors and misconceptions is helpful if the teacher understands the feedback and has the support necessary to correct the error.

*   **Feedback about the processing used in the task** is highly effective because it reminds the teacher about his or her cognitive and metacognitive thinking. For example, "I noticed that you're posting the lesson's purpose on the board and referring to it again at the end to check the students' understanding. That's giving you more information on who is getting it and who isn't."

*   **Feedback about self-regulation** is also very effective because it assists the person in self-assessing. For example, "I saw you were frustrated when the team seemed to hurry past your ideas for developing academic language. You handled it well, and when you brought it up again later in the discussion, the team was ready to listen."

*   **Feedback about the person** can be ineffective because it may not provide the person with any information about what to do next. For example, "Way to go!" may be a compliment to a team and serve a motivational purpose but does little to enable the team to engage in further reflection on its efforts.

Alternatively, noting that a member of the team persevered and was able to complete a difficult task may serve to reinforce that action and allow the person to support his or her peers in developing stamina for complex tasks.

Even the best feedback will lose its effectiveness if it is not *timely*. In addition, the feedback must be *actionable*; that is, the learner has a clear sense of direction about what he or she should do next. Feedback should also be *specific* so that the learner is equipped with a necessary level of detail about his or her next actions. Additionally, of course, it should be *understandable* in the sense that it should take into account the teacher's development. Taken together, feedback that is well-thought-out and delivered in a timely fashion will build the agency of the teacher and encourage him or her to assume more responsibility for his or her own professional learning.

Feed Forward to Inform Instruction

The process of formative assessment is incomplete unless it feeds forward into future instruction. The classroom is the unit of analysis, and the purpose of analyzing what happens in the classroom is to locate teachers who need further support and professional development. This requires some recordkeeping in order to analyze errors teachers are making. In our efforts to get to know teachers as individuals, we can lose track of patterns that are otherwise right in front of us. Call it the phenomenon of not seeing the forest for the trees. Error analysis allows us to gain a bit of perspective on who is having difficulty. For example, let's say that members of a collaborative planning team identify the lack of opportunities for student interaction as an opportunity to improve their practice and thus student learning. A simple measure might be simply tracking the number of interactions in a fifteen-minute period in ten different classrooms. This can be accomplished using teaching observations or walkthroughs with the data provided back to the collaborative planning team for analysis. The use of error analysis links back to being clear about the purpose of a collaborative team meeting; purpose statements can be used as a platform for clarifying exactly what teachers should be able to do. By creating a list of specific skills that are linked to the issue you have identified, you can not only gather evidence at the individual level but also for groups of teachers who need additional support.

In the next section, we will discuss different types of classroom visits that can become part of the repertoire of the school leader. We call them *structured walks* because each has a different purpose, and different members of the administrative and instructional staff participate in the observations. As a cautionary note, instructional rounds should be used to complement the work of collaborative teams working together to examine evidence of student learning from common assessments and making inferences about the effectiveness of instruction based on that evidence (DuFour & Marzano, 2011). Structured walks are not intended as substitutes for the teams' collaborative planning activities.

Different Classroom Observations for Different Purposes

Table 5.1 (page 82) contains a summary of different types of classroom observations. Some of these are useful for providing feedback to teachers while others allow for leaders to reflect on the implementation of professional development and collaborative planning, or of their overall PLC efforts. Still others serve an accountability function. In the examples shown in table 5.1, we provide ways to use each type of structured walk and describe how leaders can use the information to focus their efforts.

Ghost Walks

Middle school principal José Rivera uses a ghost walk to collect evidence of implementation of the school's vocabulary initiative. As part of their annual review of student performance data, the teachers notice decreasing achievement scores on the vocabulary section of the English language arts assessment. In their discussions, the teachers note that limited vocabulary knowledge is interfering with students' understanding in mathematics, science, social studies, art, and most other classes. In discussing this problem of practice, they decide to create word walls in each classroom and to focus each week on words with common prefixes, suffixes, or roots (for example, L.6–12.4b).

During a ghost walk in December following a data review that suggests vocabulary achievement is lagging behind expected levels, Principal Rivera notes that the words on the walls in over 50 percent of classrooms are unchanged from the previous month. He shares his observation at the next faculty meeting, asking teachers whether or not they think this practice is effective. He says, "I've noticed that a lot of word walls are no longer current, and I wonder about the lack of achievement we're seeing in terms of word learning. We committed to this practice as part of our school improvement efforts. Did we decide that it didn't work, or did we get too busy?" He provides time for the teachers to talk with their colleagues in their small groups and then asks the collaborative planning teams to discuss this further and make a recommendation to the whole school. When the teams report back, they suggest that teachers might have been too busy with all of the school breaks, but that they still believe in the practice and would update the word walls by the time students return from winter break. Sixth-grade teacher Malcolm Jensen comments, "The data are there in front of us, and our team needed some time to talk about it. Thank you for allowing us to talk about this. You noticed something and didn't just tell us to fix it. We talked about our beliefs, and we recommitted to our action plans."

Capacity-Building Learning Walks

The instructional leadership team (ILT)—a group of nine elected teachers and staff members, parents, and the site administrator—engages in a systematic learning walk of their elementary school. It is specifically looking for evidence of implementation of collaborative conversations, which are the focus of professional development. As part of

Table 5.1: Types of Learning Walks

Type of Walk	Purpose	Time	Participants	Follow Up After the Walk
Ghost Walks	To examine classrooms without students present to collect evidence of the school's identified problem of practice (accountability and professional development)	One hour	Principal; assistant principal; teachers; instructional leadership team (ILT); collaborative team members; central office personnel including directors, managers, and superintendents; parents; consultants; staff developers; and others as appropriate	Summary of data collected Evidence and wonderings processed with entire faculty
Capacity-Building Learning Walks (Create building leadership team first.)	To collect data for evidence of the implementation of effective practices (accountability and professional development)	One hour	Principal, assistant principal, and other members of the building leadership team	Summary of data collected Evidence and wonderings processed with entire faculty
Faculty Instructional Learning Walks	To involve entire faculty in visiting classrooms looking for evidence and collecting data around the school's identified "Problem of Practice" (accountability and professional development)	All day	Principal, assistant principal, and whoever is available each period or time segment, ultimately involving entire faculty throughout the year	Summary of data collected Evidence and wonderings processed with entire faculty
External Eyes	To provide a fresh perspective looking for evidence of identified problem of practice (look-fors) (accountability and professional development)	Two to three hours	Building principal, assistant principal, or both and outside team of principals, teachers, consultants, and so on with school members as guides	Summary of data collected Evidence and wonderings processed with entire faculty

Collaborative Administrator Walkthroughs (This may or may not be part of teacher evaluation.)	To provide positive and critical feedback regarding the target of the walk for the purpose of improvement of instruction or employment decisions (accountability and professional development)	Two to three hours	Principal and assistant principal	Individual feedback
Guided Visits (This is designed for the visiting team's learning.)	Visitors learn from the host school by viewing practices and collecting evidence to take back to their school (professional development)	Three hours	Building principal, assistant principal, or both, and small teams from other schools	Summary of data collected Evidence and wonderings for the visiting team to take away

Source: Adapted from B. McGrath, personal communication, December 14, 2012.

their analysis of the Common Core State Standards, the teachers note that students rarely engage in the types of conversation called for in the standards (for example, see SL.K–5.1). As a team, the teachers decide to make collaborative academic discussions a significant feature of their instruction. Principal Gabriel Esperanza notes, "We have to get our students talking using academic language every day in every class. If they don't engage in these types of conversations, especially using their argumentation skills, they'll never learn to write this way."

Following several professional development events and collaborative planning team meetings, the ILT designs an observation tool (see figure 5.1) and schedules its first capacity-building learning walk.

Classroom or subject:		
Teacher:		
Observers:		
Date:		
Focus strategy:		
Focus students:		
What the Teacher Says or Does	How the Students Respond	Questions I Have

Figure 5.1: Planning focus sheet for observing student interaction.

Visit **go.solution-tree.com/commoncore** for a reproducible version of this figure.

The team visits every classroom in the school over a two-hour period looking for evidence of implementation. On the team's first visit, it notes that 75 percent of teachers have students working collaboratively. In 20 percent of the classrooms, teachers are modeling and thus collaborative conversations are not appropriate, and in 5 percent of the classrooms, students are engaged in independent tasks. The team then analyzes the quality of the collaborative work, noting that students are regularly interacting using academic language but rarely asking for evidence from their peers, and they are not providing evidence for their ideas or opinions. At its next professional development session, the ILT presents its observations and invites reflection. The team shares the success with implementation, the students' use of academic language, and the level of commitment that is evident at the school. The members also note the need for additional instruction on argumentation and then invite vertical teams to meet to discuss their findings. Following thirty minutes of small-group interaction, each vertical team presents ideas for addressing the identified need. These ideas range from developing and practicing sentence frames, to video recording students using argumentation skills and then sharing with all of the classes, and to creating fishbowl conversations so that students could experience the type of collaborative conversation expected of them. What every group recommends is the development of a common formative assessment that it could use to determine current levels of student achievement. At the end of this meeting, Principal Esperanza adds, "I'd like to congratulate us on our efforts. We've done a lot in a little time, and the ILT has helped us refine this even more. I can't wait to hear from the team again about the implementation of these little fixes to make our school even better."

Faculty Instructional Learning Walks

As part of teachers' preparation period activities, a group of eight subject-area teachers and the school's assistant principal, Shayanne Douglas, engage in a faculty instructional learning walk. Their high school has been working on raising the rigor of reading materials schoolwide. The students perform very well on state achievement tests, but their achievement suffers when they take the common formative assessments based on CCSS text difficulty levels. Ninth-grade English teacher Danita Wheary says, "We want to get out in front of this so it's really up to us. There isn't much out there yet about teaching with complex texts. We want to learn from each other about how complex texts are being used."

The teachers visit nine classrooms as part of their walk, taking note of the texts in use in the classrooms and the match between the reader, the task, and the text. As they discuss their observations, the teachers agree that the difficulty levels of texts being used are indeed increasing, but there is still a ways to go. They acknowledge that it is still early in the year and that text complexity will likely continue to increase over the course of the year, but that there are still instances where the text complexity level is rather low. They share their reflections with their respective collaborative planning teams, asking their peers for ideas about what still needs to happen to raise the rigor of reading. The discussions are productive and fairly consistently centered on students' lack of vocabulary and background knowledge. Science teacher Irving Palo states, "I have to get more readings and then sequence them in such a way that the texts build conceptually on each other. I don't need to tell my students everything that they need to know before they read. Instead, I need them to develop their understanding over time as they investigate a topic through labs, readings, and interactions with their peers."

External Eyes

Five elementary school principals, all close friends, decide to schedule unannounced visits to each other's schools to provide a set of external eyes. These five schools have been working on improving their students' writing achievement and have collaborated on a number of projects, including professional development, coaching, instructional materials, and lesson plans. Every week, a couple of the principals get together and drive to another colleague's school. They walk through classrooms of teachers available at the site to look for evidence of implementation of the writing improvement plans that groups of teachers collaborating on improving student achievement developed. Following each visit, the principals provide a written summary of their observations and reflections for the principal who hosts them. Following such a visit, Principal Abel Ruffalo reads the summary aloud to the faculty and staff, thinking aloud about the meaning of comments from the visiting principals. Principal Darnell Oldman says, "It's really helpful to see my school through my colleagues' eyes. I sometimes miss things because I know this school so well. I might even make excuses, you know. Like I know that a teacher is having a hard time personally, so I might not visit that class or I might not worry about what I see if I do. My colleagues don't know that behind-the-scenes information, so I'm confronted with it. That doesn't mean that I have to address it right away, but it helps me think about it in a different way. But even more than that, when I go to visit other schools, I get a sense of what they are doing and what I *could* be doing. I really learn a lot when I visit. In fact, I think it's even more beneficial for me than for the school that hosted me."

Collaborative Administrator Walkthroughs

Collaborative administrator walkthroughs occur when site administrators observe a specific teacher together to provide feedback. In some schools, there are guidelines that administrators must follow for this observation to "count" as part of the formal evaluation process, such as giving teachers advanced notification or spending a certain amount of time in the classroom. In other locations, this is part of the expectations for site administrators, who are tasked with providing teachers with feedback about their performance. The use of observational data as part of the teacher evaluation process is described in the professional literature (see Hill, Kapitula, & Umland, 2011; Zatynski, 2012) as well as the focus on using student achievement data in evaluations (see Slotnik, 2010). As Linda Darling-Hammond, Audrey Amrein-Beardsley, Edward Haertel, and Jesse Rothstein (2012) note, "Popular modes of evaluating teachers are fraught with inaccuracies and inconsistencies" (p. 8). Evaluating teachers is not our purpose here. Rather, we are focused on collecting information that can validate and extend the instructional repertoires of teachers. As a leader—peer, coach, or administrator—your role includes leading instructional improvement efforts. As such, you have to provide teachers with feedback based on your observations. However, these observations are usually done solo. Collaborative administrative walkthroughs allow school leaders to refine their observational practices together.

Middle school principal Charmaine Stein knows this and schedules at least one classroom observation every day of the school year and makes sure that at least one of those per week is done in partnership with another administrator or instructional coach. She and her observation partner meet with teachers first to understand their instructional priorities and ascertain which students are targeted for additional instruction and intervention and discuss the observational tool they use at their school (see figure 5.2, page 88).

The week following these conversations, Principal Stein and her observation partner, Principal Margaret Fullmer, visit classrooms unannounced and record their impressions using the applicable sections of the observation tool. For example, they meet with English teacher Steve Jacobs, who is focusing on the development of characters in literary texts (for example, see RL.7.3). Principal Stein provides a summary of the instruction she observed (see figure 5.3, page 91).

At this school, the summary notes are sent electronically to teachers following the observation, and the principal schedules a time to review the notes. During their follow-up meeting, Mr. Jacobs asks, "How many times should I re-establish the purpose? I agree that I should do it more than once, but how often are you thinking?" Principal Stein and Principal Fullmer do not immediately provide a specific answer; they want to first explore his understandings. The three educators discuss the value of a clearly understood purpose and the need to review what students were learning regularly. Mr. Jacobs asks, "Do you think you could come by next week so that you can take a look and we can talk again? I really want to get this right. My students deserve it." As the conversation continues, they focus on the many positive aspects of the lesson, but Mr. Jacobs concludes, "Thank you for the compliments. I appreciate it. But I really value your honesty with what I can do to improve. I'm confident with my teaching, and I know that I can get better."

Guided Visits

Sometimes schools invite visitors from other schools to observe classroom instruction. Often, this is at the request of visitors, who want to learn about some aspect of the school and its programs. Although this is important for the visitors, it's also a great opportunity for gathering feedback from people who know less about the school and its instructional program.

Elementary school principal Patrice Washington loves to host visitors because they provide her and her staff with different perspectives. In fact, staff members believe that they became a high-performing school because they have had over five hundred "consultants" (visitors) come to provide advice about improvements, all at no cost to the school. For example, a group of fifteen teachers is visiting from a neighboring state. The teachers are interested in the student support system that the elementary school established a few years before. As part of their visit, Principal Washington asks them to notice the environmental print in each classroom. She says to the visitors, "We're trying to ensure that the walls of our classrooms also teach students. As such, we hope that the environmental print serves as a resource for students. I would appreciate it if you could let me know if we are on the right track."

Teacher:		Date:		Time:
Grade:		Course:		
Minutes into class period: (Circle one.)	0–10 10–20 20–30 30–40 40–50 50–60			

Phases of gradual release that are evident:

☐ Stating or restating content purpose, language purpose, and productive group work outcome

☐ Modeling focus lesson or metacognitive awareness using "I" statements

☐ Guided instruction during productive group work (question, probe, cue, direct explanation, and modeling)

☐ Productive group work (meaningful, interdependent collaborative group task or product)

☐ Independent learning

Focus on Curriculum: Purposes

1. Identify the posted purposes for today's lesson.

   • Content purpose:

   • Language purpose:

   • Productive group work outcome:

2. Identify the research-based components of the posted purposes. (Circle *yes* or *no*.)

Yes	No	Reflect what students will learn today		
Yes	No	Based on the benchmarks for the grade-level content area		
Yes	No	Require students to use critical or creative thinking to:		
		☐ Acquire information	☐ Resolve a problem	☐ Apply a skill	☐ Evaluate a process
Yes	No	Reflect student oral and written language needs for today's lesson		
Yes	No	Show target vocabulary or academic language frames for today's lesson		

3. Identify the type of language purpose.

a. ☐ Specialized vocabulary	☐ Technical vocabulary	
b. ☐ Structure (grammar and syntax)	☐ Structure (signal words)	☐ Structure (frames and templates)
c. ☐ Function (using language to express an opinion, summarize, persuade, question, entertain, inform, sequence, disagree, evaluate, justify, debate, and describe)		

Focus on Instruction: Modeling and Guided Instruction

1. Identify observed research-based components of teacher authentic modeling. (Circle *yes* or *no*.)

Yes	No	Consistently contains "I" statements (not "you" statements)
Yes	No	Focuses on teacher's expert thinking process (not directions) to apprentice students to teacher thinking

Yes	No	Establishes relevance of the purpose beyond the classroom or for learning's sake		
Yes	No	Includes focus on text comprehension through:		
		☐ Word solving	☐ Vocabulary	☐ Text structure	☐ Text features

2. Identify observed research-based components of teacher-guided instruction. (Circle *yes* or *no*.)

Yes	No	Purposefully differentiates instruction by scaffolding learning with all students
Yes	No	Responds to students' misconceptions or partial understanding with questions, cues, and prompts to guide learners in alleviating misconceptions

3. Determine research-based components of teacher check for understanding. (Circle *yes* or *no*.)

Yes	No	Can explain how he or she checks for understanding during and after the lesson
Yes	No	Can explain how student learning data are used to inform subsequent decisions within the current lesson and the next lesson

Focus on the Learner: Productive Group Work and Independent Learning

1. Identify grouping format.

☐ Individual	☐ Two students	☐ Three students	☐ Four students	☐ Whole class

2. Determine complexity of student work (depth of knowledge level).

☐ *4:* Extended thinking requiring complex thinking, reasoning, and planning, possibly relating concepts within or between content areas

☐ *3:* Strategic thinking requiring reasoning, developing a plan or a sequence of steps, some complexity, more than one possible answer

☐ *2:* Basic application of skills and concepts; using two or more steps for information or conceptual knowledge

☐ *1:* Recall or reproduction of a fact, information, or procedure

3. Determine if selected students can explain the following in their own words. (Circle *yes* or *no*.)

Yes	No	What they are learning
Yes	No	What they are expected to produce to demonstrate learning
Yes	No	The relevance of their learning beyond the classroom or for learning's sake

4. Determine observed research-based components of student productive group work. (Circle *yes* or *no*.)

Yes	No	Students are engaged in a relevant challenge, innovative task, or problem to solve that applies the concepts of the content purpose.
Yes	No	Students find the task challenging yet not impossible to successfully accomplish with teacher support.
Yes	No	Students have the opportunity for experimentation with concepts (not replicating what the teacher modeled).

Figure 5.2: Classroom observation tool.   continued →

Yes	No	Students use a variety of resources to experiment with concepts and apply their knowledge.
Yes	No	Students use critical or creative thinking to consolidate their learning and refine their skills.
Yes	No	Students actively interact with one another to build each other's knowledge. Indicators include body language, movement, language associated with meaningful conversations, and shared visual gaze on materials.
Yes	No	Student conversation is respectful and courteous allowing them to disagree without being disagreeable.
Yes	No	Students hold each member of the group accountable by asking questions of one another.
Yes	No	Students ask for and provide evidence to persuade or disagree, to support claims, and to reach a better understanding or consensus based on evidence and opinions others provide.
Yes	No	Students communicate using the target vocabulary or academic sentence frames.
Yes	No	Students exhibit respect for classroom resources and equipment.

5. Determine evidence of student individual accountability (structured interaction) within productive group work.

☐ Defined group-dependent roles	☐ Individual data sheet for group lab or task
☐ Collaborative data sheet, template, or chart	☐ Collaborative written task that identifies each member's contribution (for example, colors)
☐ Purposeful discussion (for example, think-pair-share or round robin)	☐ Other:

6. Determine observed research-based components of independent learning. (Circle *yes* or *no*.)

Yes	No	Students apply what they have learned to novel tasks that they understand and can successfully complete.
Yes	No	Novel tasks help students refine their skills and build their expertise.

Focus on Classroom Learning Environment

1. Determine how the classroom learning environment supports student success. (Circle *yes* or *no*.)

Yes	No	Posted models and exemplars of quality student work show expectations of purposes.
Yes	No	Scoring guides or rubrics are clearly posted in student-friendly language.
Yes	No	Routines and procedures for a safe and orderly environment are evident.
Yes	No	Routines and procedures show that students take appropriate ownership and responsibility for learning.

Source: Fisher, Frey, & Pumpian, 2012. Used with permission.

Teacher: Steve Jacobs		Date: Oct. 7		Period: 1		Lesson focus or topic: Character analysis	

Lesson structure:

X	Individual students	X	Small groups	X	Whole Class	X	ELs	X	IEP students	X	Multicultural
X	Other:										

Purpose: Mr. Jacobs posted a purpose on the wall, and he asked students to relate the purpose, understanding that their task related to character development and why they needed to attend to that.

Productive group work: Students read independently as Mr. Jacobs supported the learning of specific students in the class in a small needs-based group. As they completed the chapter, students worked in groups to analyze one of the many characters. Their task was specific and contained an individual component. Students each had a note page on which they recorded responses to specific questions related to the character. Students worked on this task for quite some time, interacting with one another about their assigned character. They selected specific descriptions from the text to describe the character and examined how this character interacted with other characters.

Independent learning: The lesson included individual reading and individual responsibility as part of the group. In addition, the entire group presented its character analysis to the rest of the class and answered questions. Each group member was required to present and speak in front of the class. When asked, the students indicated that they prefer the teacher read-alouds but that this format worked for them as well.

In both the group work and the presentations, students engaged in text-based discussions and provided evidence for their responses from the text. They understood a great deal of the complexity of the text and what motivated specific characters to act as they were. They also made connections between the character and how they predicted the story to unfold.

Recommendations: This lesson ensured that students had a strong sense of the different characters that are now integral to this text. The students were very interactive and used academic language well. The routines are clearly in place in the classroom for students to perform well.

The only recommendation we have is to return to the purpose more often. As students presented, we were thinking about how some of the comments and feedback could have included the purpose so that students fully understand why they were doing this, not only to understand the story.

Copies distributed to:

X	Teacher	X	Observer		Other:

Figure 5.3: Sample collaborative administrator walkthrough observation.

As they observe classrooms, the visitors focus on student support and how students are being tutored during the school day. They report being very impressed with what they see. In their debriefing session with Principal Washington and members of the school's instructional leadership team, the visitors note that teachers' efforts to use the walls for teaching and supporting students are paying off. One visitor says, "I can't believe how many times I saw students use the resources on the walls of the classroom. At my school, the walls are a reflection of what we've already done. At your school, they are resources for what students are doing now. You should be very proud of your efforts." Principal Washington thanks the visiting team, knowing that the teachers' needs were met and that they provided her and her staff with valuable information about their efforts.

Supporting the development of teachers as they grow in their effectiveness and efficacy is the responsibility of a school leader. This is what effective school leaders do—they anticipate challenges and put systems in place to address them. The transition to implement and assess the Common Core State Standards is going to be challenging even to the most expert teachers, so supporting teacher development is important. The best way to do this is through support of the PLC process: engaging groups of teachers in the collaborative process of determining what students have learned and what still needs to be taught.

Along the way, classroom observations can allow teachers an opportunity to see how others instruct. Teachers might take an idea here or there and use it in their classrooms. Observations can also be used to provide some context to the student learning data that collaborative planning teams consider in their discussions. That's not to say that observations are going to change student achievement in and of themselves. As Hattie (2009) emphasizes, it is not merely reflecting about teaching that impacts student learning but collective reflection from teacher *teams* "in light of evidence about their teaching" (p. 239). Educators must ultimately shift the conversation from answering "What was taught?" or "How was it taught?" to "What was learned?" and "How can we use evidence of student learning to strengthen our professional practice?" (DuFour & Marzano, 2009, p. 62). The foundational belief of PLCs is a relentless focus on student learning. The critical question to ask ourselves is not "Did we see evidence of a desired instructional practice?" but rather "Do we have evidence of student learning, and if so, which practices contribute to those outcomes?" In other words, walkthroughs should begin and end with an eye toward student learning.

What to Do When Students Struggle

Sometimes the assessment information that teachers collect will indicate that a student or group of students has failed to make progress. Sometimes this happens because the student did not receive adequate quality core instruction, perhaps due to absences or a specific teaching situation. In that case, the student needs to be retaught the content using evidence-based practices that ensure success. Sometimes students fail to make progress despite solid core instruction. In this case, the student likely needs additional supplemental instruction or intensive intervention. RTI is a system that makes instructional accommodations when students fail to progress. As with other efforts to implement the Common Core State Standards, RTI requires the mobilization of collaborative teams and entire school systems (Buffum, Mattos, & Weber, 2009).

Although RTI has become more broadly known through its inclusion in the Individuals With Disabilities Education Improvement Act of 2004, RTI has existed as a theory and practice for decades. As described in federal legislation, the intent is twofold: (1) to provide early intervention for students who are struggling and (2) to allow for an alternate means of identifying the presence of a learning disability. Unfortunately, in some schools the latter purpose has overshadowed the former. In an effort to establish a balance between the two, a growing number of states are investing in a response to instruction and intervention (RTI²) model. Before focusing on the major components of an RTI model, we will explore five mistakes that are commonly made when establishing and implementing an RTI² program.

Mistake One: Thinking Intervention, Not Instruction

An effective RTI effort begins with a quality core program—this is the first tier of the widely known three-tier model of RTI (for more information, visit the RTI Action Network at www.rtinetwork.org). A quality core program includes the kind of scaffolded learning experiences expressed through a gradual release of responsibility model of instruction (Frey & Fisher, 2010). This model includes establishing the purpose of the lesson for students, modeling one's cognitive processes by thinking aloud, and providing guided instruction through the use of questions, prompts, and cues (see page 42 for more information). In addition, students spend much of their time learning collaboratively with their peers in productive group work before attempting independent learning. Without these practices firmly in place in all classrooms, the supplemental and intensive intervention efforts of any school will be quickly overwhelmed by students who are failing simply because they are not receiving quality core instruction.

One of the most important characteristics of Tier 1 is that all students have access to grade-level standards. A school can provide every student with effective initial instruction, but if some students are removed from essential grade-level core curriculum, and instead are "tracked" in remedial coursework, these students will not learn at high levels. Considering the required rigor of the CCSS, schools may be tempted to remove the most at-risk students from this demanding curriculum and justify the practice by claiming that they are following the RTI practice of differentiating in Tier 1.

Mistake Two: Relying on Prepackaged Curricula

While commercial programs labeled as being intervention friendly can provide some needed practice materials, they cannot replace well-designed and individualized lessons targeting the specific needs of students who require support. Typically, these programs simply provide students with practice that consists of feedback on correct and incorrect responses. Although practice is important, students who struggle with reading and writing need someone to analyze their error patterns and then provide instruction.

Callie is fortunate to attend a high school that has avoided this error. "We used to drag all the Tier 2 students through the same reading program, regardless of their needs," says reading specialist Katherine Rodas. "Now I align my materials with what students are using in their content classrooms. I also work with my collaborative planning team to diagnose *why* she is struggling. When we get to the causes, we can really help her learn and not just treat the symptom," she says.

Callie, who struggles with reading comprehension, reads passages from her science and history textbooks, as well as other related texts. Ms. Rodas comments, "I know from talking with Mr. Fitz, one of Callie's teachers, that her class is working on argumentative essays right now, so the vocabulary and reading work that we're doing together is about that." Ms. Rodas counts on regular communication with the other teachers to design lessons that are meaningful.

Mistake Three: Isolating Teachers and Interventionists

Coordinating learning across the school day is challenging under the best of circumstances, and adding intervention efforts to the mix can be difficult. It can be tempting to simply put one teacher in charge of an RTI program, give him or her a classroom, and turn attention to other matters. But isolating interventionists from classroom teachers severely limits the kind of collaboration Mr. Fitz and Ms. Rodas are able to accomplish for Callie's benefit. Instead, consider the collaborative planning team effort each student in an RTI[2] program will need to be successful. It is important to make sure that every student receiving supplemental instruction or intensive interventions has an identified person to coordinate instruction and another to coordinate intervention. Communication between these two educators can bridge the divide that can otherwise occur when interventions are disconnected from the core curriculum.

Mistake Four: Making Data Decisions Alone

Ms. Rodas, the reading specialist, collects data each time she meets with a student so that she can track progress and determine what is working. Importantly, data collection and analysis also reveal when something is not working.

"I initially started out with using timed writing with her, but I quickly discovered that wasn't the best approach. I found that when I gave her a chance to discuss the reading with me for a few minutes first, her writing improved in length and content. I've talked with my collaborative planning team members, and we have been able to spot a lot of trends in her performance," says Ms. Rodas.

Both Mr. Fitz and Ms. Rodas serve on the school's RTI[2] subcommittee, an outgrowth of the Student Study Team formed to closely examine the circumstances surrounding specific students' behavioral or academic difficulties. The subcommittee meets in response to the work teachers do in their collaborative planning teams to review the progress of students receiving intervention supports. Of course, the collaborative planning teams are discussing students' performance and instructional needs on a continuous basis. The RTI[2] subcommittee provides another set of eyes that allows for trends across all of the teams.

Ms. Rodas brings her data to the group for discussion and finds that others can sometimes spot a trend she has overlooked. In addition, she can share her insights about what she has found effective. For instance, she recommends that Mr. Fitz and Callie's other teachers have the students plan their writing orally in advance of extended writing assignments.

"I'm trying to do this more often, not just with Callie but with several others," Mr. Fitz observes. "I make sure that she gets a chance to talk with a small group of peers, and I'm beginning to see how she's organizing her thinking. It's showing up on her papers."

Mistake Five: Leaving the Family Out of the Planning

Family involvement is an important consideration in RTI[2] efforts. The family may possess quite a bit of information that can help determine ways to accelerate student learning. As keepers of their child's history, family members have firsthand knowledge about what has worked in the past. However, this information can come too late in the process when families are contacted only after a student's lack of RTI warrants a referral for special education testing. Understandably, families can become frustrated when they learn that their child has been involved in an intervention for months without their knowledge.

At Callie's school, her mother and stepfather initially met with Duane Demar, the administrator who oversees the RTI[2] program. He explained why their daughter was being recommended for supplemental intervention and gathered information from them about past efforts. Now, Ms. Rodas speaks with them on the phone each month to share Callie's progress and ask them about their observations. While Callie's eventual progress means she doesn't require a referral for special education testing, the school has gained two important allies.

"I thought the only time you heard from the school was when there was a problem," says Callie's mother. "But we were treated with much respect. It mattered what we knew."

This is not to say that all parents are currently capable of providing this level of support. Schools can be quite successful in raising achievement even when parents do not have the time, skills, or motivation to engage with the school system. However, it's good practice to invite parents into the process of their child's education.

Response to Instruction and Intervention

With all the debate about the effects of accountability systems, one element is held in wide agreement: necessary attention is finally drawn to the progress of students with special needs. The shorthand of accountability-speak is that these students comprise *significant subgroups*: students whose socioeconomic, ethnic, linguistic, and learning differences warrant our attention. However, any school leader knows that the broad categories of significant subgroups can obscure the specific needs of each student. In this section, we will discuss topics related to instruction and intervention. We begin with discussion about the curricular and personnel elements involved at each tier of an RTI[2] system. We will then describe variables that can be manipulated to devise an effective RTI[2] system at your school.

RTI[2] seeks to prevent the *waiting to fail* model that does a disservice to students who otherwise must demonstrate a significant skill deficit before receiving valuable supplemental instruction. It is also used as an alternative means for qualifying students with special needs for special education services. These two purposes are sometimes aligned and sometimes not. Like any educational practice, RTI² can be done well, badly, or somewhere in between. When done poorly, RTI² puts a student through a perfunctory supplemental program that is not tailored to his or her unique strengths and needs, then the student is rapidly qualified for special education services, where he or she is viewed as "someone else's problem." When RTI² is done well, students and families are fully involved in a responsive system of supplemental instruction and intensive intervention that is customized to meet the student's needs. Special education qualification is available only if and when it is needed to further the student's education.

RTI is most commonly represented as a three-tiered approach (see figure 5.4). Tier 1 describes a quality core program, based on grade-level standards in English language arts that all students receive. This is where good first teaching occurs and is the first place where adjustments to practice should occur in order to increase effectiveness. As a school leader, this is the first place to look for problems of practice and student achievement. If 70–80 percent of the students at your school are not approaching, meeting, or exceeding grade-level expectations, then the core program needs improvement.

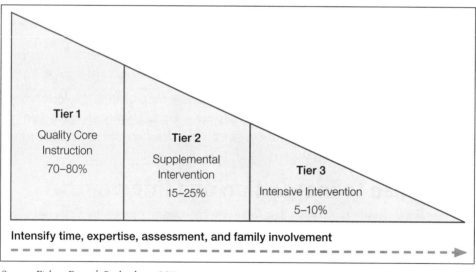

Tier 1
Quality Core
Instruction
70–80%

Tier 2
Supplemental
Intervention
15–25%

Tier 3
Intensive Intervention
5–10%

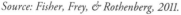
Intensify time, expertise, assessment, and family involvement

Source: Fisher, Frey, & Rothenberg, 2011.

Figure 5.4: Distribution of RTI supports.

Tier 2 describes supplemental intervention. The word *supplemental* is key. Instruction at this level is in addition to, not a replacement of, quality core instruction. Therefore, Tier 2 should not replace a student's access to quality core instruction. In some cases, the classroom teacher can deliver Tier 2 intervention, especially if the rest of the class is engaged in collaborative learning or extension activities. Other personnel may be involved in supplemental instruction, depending on the structure of the collaborative planning team. For example, all third-grade students who are struggling with fluency, as data from a common formative assessment demonstrate, might receive Tier 2 intervention from a teacher who is the team's expert in this intervention. Typically, it is not practical to have more than 15–25 percent of the students at a school involved in supplemental interventions. These supplemental interventions often come in the form of additional small-group instruction that guides students toward greater understanding of core content.

Tier 3 intensive intervention is reserved for students who have not demonstrated progress in Tier 2 or who are significantly delayed as evidenced on initial screening tools. Typically delivered daily and individually, Tier 3 instruction is designed to increase the intensity of the intervention. Manipulating several variables including frequency, duration, group size, or training of the person delivering the intervention is an example of how to increase the intensity of Tier 3 interventions. Regardless, Tier 3 must be targeted interventions that are developed based on diagnostic assessments. By way of example, Reading Recovery (http://readingrecovery.org) is a Tier 3 intensive intervention for first-grade students. Because of the one-to-one instruction, other personnel are often involved, and it is commonly delivered outside the grade-level classroom. The heightened degree of services limits Tier 3 supports to approximately 5–10 percent of the school population. All of these percentages should be taken under advisement, as the unique nature of schools, staffing, and resources impacts a school's ability to offer a responsive intervention program.

Tier 1: Quality Core Instruction

In chapter 3, we discussed the instructional features of quality instruction through a gradual release of responsibility model. You will recall that these four features include the following (Fisher & Frey, 2008).

1. Purpose and modeling to focus lessons

2. Guided instruction using robust questions, prompts, and cues

3. Productive group work to inspire collaborative learning

4. Independent learning both in class and out of school

However, instruction is meaningless without curriculum. A central assumption of effective instruction is that the teacher understands the cultural, linguistic, and experiential differences between and among his or her students. The research on culturally responsive teaching is extensive (see Gay, 2000; Moll, Amanti, Neff, & González, 1992; Suárez-Orozco, Suárez-Orozco, & Todorova, 2008). In any quality core program, the curriculum is crafted to build on the collective strengths of the learners in order to expand their knowledge of the world around them. Geneva Gay (2000) calls this *culturally responsive teaching* and advises that careful preparations are necessary to do so. These include becoming culturally aware, designing culturally relevant curriculum, building a learning community, and fostering cross-cultural communication.

A quality core program provides purposeful teaching and scaffolded instruction within a strong standards-based curriculum that builds on experiences while broadening and deepening students' understanding of the world. It is a tall order, but a necessary one for effective English language arts instruction. Quality indicators to look for in Tier 1 include the following.

- **Time:** Time is devoted each day to English language arts instruction that is aligned with grade-level standards. States and districts vary on the number of instructional minutes, but typically this requires at least sixty to ninety minutes of literacy instruction daily.

- **Expertise:** Expertise comes in the form of a highly qualified teacher who designs and implements research-based curriculum aligned with the state standards. The curriculum utilizes paraprofessionals and volunteers strategically to enhance the program.

- **Group size:** Group size is variable, depending on the phase of instruction. A gradual release of responsibility model of instruction includes whole-class, small-group, and individual instruction.

- **Assessment:** Assessment occurs at least three times per year in the form of benchmark assessments. These results are used to inform subsequent instruction, form groups, and identify areas of the curriculum that require reteaching.

- **Family involvement:** Family involvement includes providing information about the core program in a variety of forums, including curriculum night, parent-teacher conferences, family literacy events, and classroom newsletters. Family organizations are actively involved in these efforts, including outreach to the broader community.

Tier 2: Supplemental Intervention

When students fail to make progress with the quality core curriculum, it is necessary to offer supplemental instruction. In the language of RTI², this is Tier 2. The intended effect of Tier 2 is to provide a double dose of instruction in order to make Tier 1 more accessible. Therefore, Tier 2 lessons are likely to be used to build background knowledge, frontload content, expand vocabulary knowledge, or reteach essential grade-level standards when Tier 1 has not been effective. Because the purpose is to supplement Tier 1 instruction—not supplant it—these lessons should be closely tied to the curriculum taught in the quality core program. For this reason, separate prepackaged Tier 2 programs are not especially useful for students who struggle. For a student who is already having difficulty with the original curriculum, having the teacher introduce a second unrelated one will result in more confusion.

Tier 2 supplemental intervention can be delivered within the classroom in order to capitalize on the momentum established during core instruction. In practical terms, this means additional small-group instruction for Tier 2 students. Tier 2 is also often implemented through the use of additional time structures, such as study skills classes, homework help, study halls, or supplemental intervention provided while other students are in enrichment activities (Buffum et al., 2009). The benefits of small-group instruction are significant for all learners (see Hattie, 2009, for a detailed meta-analysis), and this is especially true for students who struggle. An effective quality core program in English language arts should include daily small-group instruction as a matter of form. Students identified for Tier 2 receive additional small-group instruction before school, during school, or after school—essentially whenever it can be accomplished. The key is that participation is not optional or invitational; it is mandatory and scheduled. While students performing at grade level may be meeting twice a week in teacher-directed small groups, Tier 2–identified students might meet four to five times a week.

However, you should exercise caution regarding the personnel you use to implement Tier 2 supplemental intervention—expertise is key. Some schools are fortunate to have paraprofessionals and volunteers available to enrich the classrooms. These men and women are valuable in so many ways, especially in being able to provide students with the attention and caring they deserve. However, these same people are taxed beyond their scope of knowledge when they are asked to deliver Tier 2 intervention. Students who struggle should have access to more, not less, expertise. Therefore, the collaborative planning team should comprise experts, and the teachers on the team should meet with Tier 2 groups. This is an ideal time for paraprofessionals and volunteers to work with the rest of the class while the teacher meets with the Tier 2 group.

While the classroom teacher is delivering instruction, the consultative support of other specialists on the collaborative planning team is a welcome addition for supplemental interventions. Look at the resources you have at your school. Do you have an instructional coach? A bilingual specialist? A reading coach? These and other specialists can contribute valuable ideas and assessments to the ongoing conversation about supporting learners in Tier 2. While these professionals are often eager to share with their colleagues, finding time to do so is often hard. As a school leader, creating schedules that allow for these consultative relationships to bloom should be a top priority. It is amazing to witness the problem-solving capacity of groups when given the time and resources to do so.

The size of Tier 2 groups is important. Because the purpose of Tier 2 supplemental intervention is to build needed skills and abilities for Tier 1, these groups should be very small in size—no more than three or four students. The number is not arbitrary. Sharon Vaughn and Silvia Linan-Thompson (2003) examine the effects of an elementary reading intervention and find that groups of three have a strong positive effect on learning, while larger groups of ten do not. Additionally, supplemental intervention often involves oral language use, and increasing the number of students decreases the number of interaction opportunities. In some secondary schools, supplemental interventions are built into a supplemental class, either during the school day or after, thus allowing students to work in small groups with a teacher and engage in practice and review when they are not with the teacher.

Tier 2 supplemental intervention also requires intensification of assessment. In addition to the benchmark assessments of a quality core program, students in Tier 2 should be assessed at least once or twice a month to more closely monitor their progress. These assessments need not be time-consuming, but they should measure what is being taught. Therefore, timed writing assessments, a measure of vocabulary acquisition, or a comprehension assessment of a reading passage may be warranted. Most importantly, the results should be used to inform subsequent instruction, not simply measure skills. Without the flexibility to make midcourse corrections, teachers feel justifiably frustrated. Keep the term in mind: *response to intervention*. An overarching goal is to find what works and then use that information to benefit the learner.

In the rush to provide supplemental instruction, teachers and leaders can easily overlook the family's involvement. It is vital that families feel informed and comfortable with the process, especially when their child is showing early signs of struggle. In some districts, parent liaisons may be able to offer additional assistance or guidance about fostering family participation. You may consider offering meetings off campus at a mutually agreed-on location. This may put the family at ease and allow family members to participate more fully in the discussion. It is also essential to keep in mind that these are not one-way conversations. The family often knows much more about what has been successful with their child, and their insights can be of much value in designing effective supplemental instruction.

Supplemental instruction for English learners should be tied to the quality core program, and should focus on one or more broad practices, including building background knowledge, frontloading content, and expanding vocabulary and conceptual understanding. However, these should not be offered in isolation from other curricular connections. Students should have the opportunity to learn and practice these skills within the context of what they are learning in the core program. Quality indicators to look for in Tier 2 include the following.

- **Time:** Time is dedicated to supplemental instruction at least three times per week and daily if possible.

- **Expertise:** Expertise is ensured because the teacher is the main point of contact for instruction. Paraprofessionals and volunteers support the other students in the class during this time. In addition, the teacher also has consultative access to school-based experts, including coaches, specialists, special educators, and other related-services personnel who can provide needed interventions for targeted students. This is an important role of the collaborative planning team—teachers support each other and offer their expertise in providing supports for students.

- **Group size:** Group size is reduced to make sure that students have many opportunities to respond and participate. For this reason, the group should consist of three to four students at the most. Other factors may reduce the size of the group. Younger students may benefit from an even smaller group size.

- **Assessment:** Assessment should occur once or twice a month to monitor progress and inform instruction. These assessments need not be time-consuming but should be aligned with the instruction offered.

- **Family involvement:** Family involvement should occur before, not after the fact. When concerns arise about a student's lack of progress, the family should be informed. This can occur either in or out of school. Keep in mind that information should flow both ways. Remember to solicit insights and recommendations from the family.

Tier 3: Intensive Intervention

A smaller number of students need intensive intervention. To use the language of the Illinois Alliance for School-Based Problem-Solving and Intervention Resources in Education (ASPIRE), while Tier 2 is about providing more support, Tier 3 is about offering the most support for students to be successful. This means intensifying time, expertise, group size, assessment, and family involvement to design an intervention that is targeted diagnostically to the cause of the student's learning issue. RTI efforts fail when they are not aligned with a clear diagnosis of the problem and instead focus on generic skill development. The goal is to ensure that the student can benefit from the quality core program, but he or she does not necessarily need to be performing at grade level to do so. Keep in mind that differentiation is a part of effective core instruction.

While it is not possible (or even advisable) to predict what the content of a Tier 3 intervention might look like for a given student, we can look to the research about this level of support for elementary students. Jeanne Wanzek and Sharon Vaughn (2010) review studies on Tier 3 reading interventions. For kindergarten through grade 3, they draw the following conclusions.

- The most effective interventions combine meaningful text reading with skills instruction, especially phonics.

- The best results are from one-to-one instruction, with groups showing smaller gains.

- The earlier the intervention is applied, the better. Results in kindergarten and first grade are higher than those in second and third grades.

They draw the following conclusions for grades 4–5.

- The most effective interventions emphasize reading comprehension and vocabulary. Fluency interventions have mixed results.

- Multicomponent interventions that include a mix of reading comprehension instruction, vocabulary, and some fluency and phonics instruction are effective.

- Thirty-minute one-to-one intervention models work well when combined with curricular emphases identified previously—reading comprehension, vocabulary, fluency, and phonics.

Research on Tier 3 interventions for middle and high school students is less robust than those designed for elementary learners. However, the research evidence using the broader lens of struggling adolescent readers is more extensive. Sharon Vaughn and Jack Fletcher (2012) summarize the findings from this body of research in grades 6–12.

- Adolescence is not too late to intervene. Interventions do benefit older students. However, complex reading–related problems, such as vocabulary development and background knowledge that are associated with comprehension, are unlikely to be readily and quickly remediated.

- Consider the type of reading problem (for example, word level, text or background knowledge level, or a combination of these factors), and focus the treatment to meet students' needs. Older students with reading difficulties benefit from interventions focused at both the word and the text level.

- Most older students with reading difficulties benefit from improved knowledge about concepts and vocabulary related to their content learning.

- Since background knowledge and vocabulary are considerably underdeveloped in the vast majority of older students with reading difficulties, schoolwide approaches to enhancing knowledge and vocabulary across Tier 1 content areas (for example, social studies, science, math, and reading and language arts) are needed.

- Teaching comprehension strategies to older students with reading difficulties is beneficial but is likely insufficient for students who also have significant difficulties with vocabulary, background knowledge, or decoding.

- The reading comprehension gains of students in grades 6 to 12 are likely to be significantly smaller than those in other reading and reading-related areas including foundation skills such as phonemic awareness and phonics.

- We can expect that remediation of students with significant reading problems who are in grades 6 to 12 is likely to take several years.

Because of the intensive nature of a Tier 3 intervention, it is often impractical to offer such supports within the classroom. Therefore, schools often offer this level of intervention elsewhere in the school or in supplemental classes. Additionally, often an expert other than the classroom teacher—a coach, specialist, or special education teacher—delivers the intervention. However, the limited time available to this small cadre of educators may strain the resources of the school. Therefore, every certificated adult without classroom responsibilities should provide instruction to one or two students (Fisher, Frey, & Rothenberg, 2011). This arrangement increases our capacity to offer intensive intervention to more students who need it, while shifting some of the workload away from the limited number of specialists in the school.

An effective program offers opportunities for differentiated instruction, supplemental instruction, and intensive intervention daily. Keep in mind that the name of the game at this level is *most*, and it's definitely not time to hold anything back in our arsenal of good instructional practice. The evidence on the value of one-to-one instruction with a highly qualified teacher is strong (Frey, 2006), especially because this arrangement makes it possible to respond immediately to any difficulties or confusions that the learner is experiencing. However, this is not always practical, and schools can manipulate a number of different variables such as duration, frequency, expertise of staff, and targeted skills to develop and implement an effective Tier 3 intervention.

In Tier 3 intervention, the collaborative planning team closely tracks progress, which is often measured through specific skills tests called curriculum-based measures (CBMs). These tests are generally fluency based, of short duration, and meant to serve as a proxy for progress in a curriculum area. Most importantly, CBMs are normed so that a comparison can be made to expected levels of achievement. For example, there are CBMs in reading that include alphabet naming and timed oral fluency and writing measures. Typically, the CBMs are focused on foundational skills, such as phonemic awareness, phonics, spelling, and fluency (for example, see RF.K–5.1–4). Leaders should be aware what CBMs their schools use, what the results of the CBMs mean, and how to support collaborative planning teams in responding to the results of these measures.

Curriculum-based assessments (CBAs) are also effective ways to monitor progress. These are tests that use the school materials and curriculum as the basis of measurement. Although they lack the technical robustness of CBMs, curriculum-based assessments offer the advantage of a more direct link to what is being taught. For example, a student's progress through an English unit on poetry is a curriculum-based assessment. The CBAs are directly linked with the Common Core State Standards in that formative assessments based on the standards provide information to collaborative planning teams about student success and needs for intervention. Leaders should evaluate the quality of the CBAs that teachers are using, determine whether the CBAs are aligned with the Common Core State Standards, and support collaborative planning teams in responding to the results of these assessments.

Tier 3 intensive intervention is reserved for students who have failed to make progress through supplemental intervention. The goal is to elevate the student's skills so that he or she can benefit from the quality core program. Because Tier 3 results can be used for special education referral, it is vital that the measurements used are valid and reliable. In addition, the family's role deepens. Because RTI² is essentially a problem-solving process, it is essential to gain the full participation of the family. Because learning happens both at home and at school, an RTI² effort that leaves the family out of the equation is a diminished and less effective one. Quality indicators to look for in Tier 3 include the following.

- **Time:** Time in intervention is increased to daily sessions of at least 30 minutes. Younger students may need a period of time to adjust due to stamina. Older students might be involved in this type of intervention for 90 or 120 minutes.

- **Expertise:** Expertise is further expanded to include specialists and coaches for direct instruction. In schools with a large number of Tier 3 students, every certificated adult (administrators, librarians, and so on) has a caseload of one or more students.

- **Group size:** Group size is decreased in order to maximize responsive teaching.

- **Assessment:** Assessments in the form of curriculum-based measurements and curriculum-based assessments are collected and analyzed weekly to monitor progress and make instructional decisions.

- **Family involvement:** Family involvement is further intensified, and parents are recruited to be members of the problem-solving team.

- **Intervention teams:** Intervention teams are an important aspect of Tier 3 intervention. Teams have specific expertise and training and are created as collaborative problem solvers that can assist in intervention efforts. Given the extensive needs of students at Tier 3, teams that focus on intervention can help ensure that students receive the support they need to be successful.

Table 5.2 presents a summary of the differences between Tier 1, Tier 2, and Tier 3 in terms of use of time, access to expertise, group size, assessment, and family involvement.

Conclusion

Leading a school through the change process required to implement the Common Core State Standards cannot be accomplished through sheer will alone, nor is it a solitary task. The key to complex change is to empower teachers, students, and families to participate more fully in the business of school. School leaders can accomplish this engagement through the PLC process. This means leaders need to design processes and procedures that allow teachers to regularly interact with their peers and answer the guiding questions of a collaborative planning team: What do we want our students to learn? How will we know when they have learned it? How will we respond when some students don't learn? How will we extend and enrich the learning for students who are already proficient? The PLC process is powerful because of the feedback and learning that result from high-functioning collaborative teams. This collaborative work is even more important than ever as leaders are charged with shepherding their schools through this period of transition to the Common Core State Standards.

An effective school leader anticipates the supports students will need. In adopting the Common Core State Standards, we are collectively saying that we believe in increasing the rigor of our lessons. But it also means that more students than ever before will

Table 5.2: Matrix of an Effective Response to Instruction and Intervention (RTI²) Program

	Tier 1: Quality Core Instruction	Tier 2: Supplemental Instruction	Tier 3: Intensive Intervention
Time	Teachers deliver instruction daily for at least sixty to ninety minutes.	Supplemental instruction should occur at least three times a week, in addition to the quality core program.	Intensive intervention occurs daily, for at least thirty minutes per session in grades K–5 and 90 to 120 minutes for grades 6–12.
Expertise	The classroom teacher designs and delivers research-based instruction using standards-aligned curriculum.	The classroom teacher delivers instruction in consultation with other school-based experts and his or her collaborative planning team.	A specialist primarily delivers instruction. At schools where large numbers of Tier 3 students attend, all certificated personnel have a caseload.
Group Size	Classes offer a mixture of whole-class, small-group, and individual instruction using a gradual release of responsibility model that includes purpose and modeling, guided instruction, productive group work, and independent learning.	Classes are restricted to groups of no more than three to four students. Teachers consider age, language proficiency, and instructional purpose when determining group size.	Instruction is one-to-one and individualized to meet the needs of the learner.
Assessment	Teachers collect and analyze benchmark assessments at least three times per year. They use results to fine-tune instructional and curricular decisions with their collaborative planning teams.	Teachers collect assessment information one to two times per month that mirrors what is being taught. They use results to inform subsequent instruction.	Teachers use CBMs and CBAs carefully to consider grade-level expectations and compare students with true peers, such as English learners who have similar years of English education. Assessment occurs weekly.
Family Involvement	Families have many outlets for understanding the quality core program, including curriculum nights, teacher conferences, classroom newsletters, community outreach, and parent organizations.	Teachers and leaders involve families in the process of identification and progress monitoring. They are informed monthly about their child's progress and subsequent instructional decisions.	Families are fully involved in the process and are seen as fellow problem solvers.

Intensify time, expertise, assessment, and family involvement

Source: Fisher & Frey, 2012.

struggle. Thus, a response to intervention system must be purposeful, strategic, and equally rigorous. Like other aspects of the change process, these systems cannot be implemented by a few individuals while the rest of the people stand by. A schoolwide investment in intervention is required if it is to succeed. More than ever before, these efforts must involve all stakeholders, including general and special education staff, specialists, and families. By leading change in partnership with all members of the school community, we can reach the goal of truly preparing students for college and careers.

REFERENCES AND RESOURCES

Alig-Mielcarek, J. M., & Hoy, W. K. (2005). Instructional leadership: Its nature, meaning, and influence. In C. G. Miskel & W. K. Hoy (Eds.), *Educational leadership and reform* (pp. 29–52). Greenwich, CT: Information Age.

American Speech-Language-Hearing Association. (2012). *What is language? What is speech?* Accessed at www.asha.org/public/speech/development/language_speech.htm on September 26, 2012.

Aud, S., Hussar, W., Kena, G., Bianco, K., Frohlich, L., Kemp, J., & Tahan, K. (2011). *The condition of education 2011: Indicator 6—Children who spoke a language other than English at home* (NCES 2011-033). Washington, DC: U.S. Government Printing Office. Accessed at http://nces.ed.gov/programs/coe/pdf/coe_lsm.pdf on December 18, 2012.

Bandura, A. (1965). Influence of models' reinforcement contingencies on the acquisition of imitative responses. *Journal of Personality and Social Psychology, 1*(6), 589–595.

Bandura, A. (1977). *Social learning theory.* Englewood Cliffs, NJ: Prentice Hall.

Bass, B. M. (1985). Leadership: Good, better, best. *Organizational Dynamics, 13*(3), 26–40.

Baumann, J. F., Font, G., Edwards, E. C., & Boland, E. (2005). Strategies for teaching middle-grade students to use word-part and context clues to expand reading vocabulary. In E. H. Hiebert & M. L. Kamil (Eds.), *Teaching and learning vocabulary: Bringing research to practice.* Mahwah, NJ: Erlbaum.

Beck, I. L., McKeown, M. G., & Kucan, L. (2002). *Bring words to life: Robust vocabulary instruction.* New York: Guilford Press.

Beck, I. L., McKeown, M. G., & Kucan, L. (2008). *Creating robust vocabulary: Frequently asked questions and extended examples.* New York: Guilford Press.

Berninger, V. M., & Abbott, R. D. (2010). Listening comprehension, oral expression, reading comprehension, and written expression: Related yet unique language systems in grades 1, 3, 5, and 7. *Journal of Educational Psychology, 102*(3), 635–651.

Bettebenner, D. W., & Linn, R. L. (2010). *Growth in student achievement: Issues of measurement, longitudinal data analysis, and accountability.* Paper presented at the Exploratory Seminar: Measurement Challenges Within the Race to the Top Agenda, Austin, TX. Accessed at www.k12center.org/rsc/pdf /BetebennerandLinnPresenterSession1.pdf on December 14, 2012.

Birenbaum, M., Kimron, H., & Shilton, H. (2011). Nested contexts that shape assessment for learning: School-based professional learning community and classroom culture. *Studies in Educational Evaluation, 37*(1), 35–48.

Blachowicz, C. L. Z., & Fisher, P. (2002). *Teaching vocabulary in all classrooms* (2nd ed.). Upper Saddle River, NJ: Merrill/Prentice Hall.

Blase, J., & Blase, J. (1999). Principals' instructional leadership and teacher development: Teachers' perspectives. *Educational Administration Quarterly, 35*(3), 349–378.

Boaler, J., William, D., & Brown, M. (2000). Students' experiences of ability grouping—disaffection, polarisation and the construction of failure. *British Educational Research Journal, 26*(5), 631–648.

Broussard, C. A., & Joseph, A. L. (1998). Tracking: A form of educational neglect? *Social Work in Education, 20*(2), 110–120.

Buffum, A., Mattos, M., & Weber, C. (2009). *Pyramid response to intervention: RTI, professional learning communities, and how to respond when kids don't learn.* Bloomington, IN: Solution Tree Press.

Bullough, R. V., Jr., & Baugh, S. C. (2008). Building professional learning communities within a university–public school partnership. *Theory Into Practice, 47*(4), 286–293.

Buswell, B. E., Schaffner, C. B., & Seyler, A. B. (Eds.). (1999). *Opening doors: Connecting students to curriculum, classmates, and learning* (2nd ed.). Colorado Springs, CO: PEAK Parent Center.

Center for K–12 Assessment and Performance Management. (2012). *The five new multi-state assessment systems under development.* Washington, DC: Educational Testing Service. Accessed at www.k12center.org/publications/all .html?WT.ac=17559_1109_publications on September 26, 2012.

Center for Research on the Context of Teaching. (2002). *Bay area school reform collaborative: Phase one (1995–2001) evaluation.* Stanford, CA: Stanford University.

Chall, J. S., & Jacobs, V. A. (2003). Poor children's fourth-grade slump. *American Educator, 27*(1), 14–15, 44.

Cohen, E. G., & Miller, R. H. (1980). Coordination and control of instruction in schools. *The Pacific Sociological Review, 23*(4), 446–473.

Council of Chief State School Officers. (2012a, January 26). *The Common Core State Standards: Supporting districts and teachers with text complexity* [Webinar]. Accessed at https://ccsso.webex.com/mw0306ld/mywebex/default.do;jsessioni d=KGRNPd6hnnshndyz9QLk5qthTtFvV6yPkQTTPg2XGvZ489Lm2pTQ! 1006560109?nomenu=true&siteurl=ccsso&service=6&rnd=0.8424170944354 614&main_url=https%3A%2F%2Fccsso.webex.com%2Fec0605ld%2Feventc enter%2Fprogram%2FprogramDetail.do%3FtheAction%3Ddetail%26siteurl %3Dccsso%26cProgViewID%3D22 on May 24, 2012.

Council of Chief State School Officers. (2012b). *Framework for English language proficiency development standards corresponding to the Common Core State Standards and the Next Generation Science Standards.* Washington, DC: Author.

Creasap, S., Peters, A., & Uline, C. (2005). The effects of guided reflection on educational leadership practice: Mentoring and portfolio writing as a means to transformative learning for early-career principals. *The Journal of School Leadership, 15*(4), 352–386.

Darling-Hammond, L. (2010). *The flat world and education: How America's commitment to equity will determine our future.* New York: Teachers College Press.

Darling-Hammond, L., Amrein-Beardsley, A., Haertel, E., & Rothstein, J. (2012). Evaluating teacher evaluation. *Phi Delta Kappan, 93*(6), 8–15.

DiPaola, M. F., & Hoy, W. K. (2008). *Principals improving instruction: Supervision, evaluation, and professional development.* Boston: Pearson Education.

Downey, C. J., Steffy, B. E., English, F. W., Frase, L. E., & Poston, W. K. (2004). *The three-minute classroom walk-through: Changing school supervisory practice one teacher at a time.* Thousand Oaks, CA: Corwin Press.

DuFour, R., DuFour, R., & Eaker, R. (2008). *Revisiting professional learning communities at work: New insights for improving schools.* Bloomington, IN: Solution Tree Press.

DuFour, R., DuFour, R., Eaker, R., & Karhanek, G. (2010). *Raising the bar and closing the gap: Whatever it takes.* Bloomington, IN: Solution Tree Press.

DuFour, R., DuFour, R., Eaker, R., & Many, T. (2006). *Learning by doing: A handbook for professional learning communities at work.* Bloomington, IN: Solution Tree Press.

DuFour, R., DuFour, R., Eaker, R., & Many, T. (2010). *Learning by doing: A handbook for professional learning communities at work* (2nd ed.). Bloomington, IN: Solution Tree Press.

DuFour, R., & Marzano, R. J. (2009). How teachers learn: High-leverage strategies for principal leadership. *Educational Leadership, 66*(5), 62–68.

DuFour, R., & Marzano, R. J. (2011). *Leaders of learning: How district, school, and classroom leaders improve student achievement.* Bloomington, IN: Solution Tree Press.

Duke, N. K., & Pearson, P. D. (2002). Effective practices for developing reading comprehension. In A. E. Farstrup & S. J. Samuels (Eds.), *What research has to say about reading instruction* (pp. 205–242). Newark, DE: International Reading Association.

Eaker, R., DuFour, R., & DuFour, R. (2002). *Getting started: Reculturing schools to become professional learning communities.* Bloomington, IN: Solution Tree Press.

FairTest Examiner. (2008). *Changes to state assessment systems.* Accessed at www .fairtest.org/changes-state-assessment-systems on December 14, 2012.

Fisher, D., Brozo, W. G., Frey, N., & Ivey, G. (2011). *50 instructional routines to develop content literacy* (2nd ed.). Boston: Allyn & Bacon.

Fisher, D., & Frey, N. (2001). Access to the core curriculum: Critical ingredients for student success. *Remedial and Special Education, 22*(3), 148–157.

Fisher, D., & Frey, N. (2007). *Checking for understanding: Formative assessment techniques for your classroom.* Alexandria, VA: Association for Supervision and Curriculum Development.

Fisher, D., & Frey, N. (2008). *Better learning through structured teaching: A framework for the gradual release of responsibility.* Alexandria, VA: Association for Supervision and Curriculum Development.

Fisher, D., & Frey, N. (2010). *Guided instruction: How to develop confident and successful learners.* Alexandria, VA: Association for Supervision and Curriculum Development.

Fisher, D., & Frey, N. (2011). *The purposeful classroom: How to structure lessons with learning goals in mind.* Alexandria, VA: Association for Supervision and Curriculum Development.

Fisher, D., & Frey, N. (2012). *The school leader's guide to English learners.* Bloomington, IN: Solution Tree Press.

Fisher, D., Frey, N., & Lapp, D. (2008). *In a reading state of mind: Brain research, teacher modeling, and comprehension instruction.* Newark, DE: International Reading Association.

Fisher, D., Frey, N., & Lapp, D. (2011). Focusing on the participation and engagement gap: A case study on closing the achievement gap. *Journal of Education for Students Placed at Risk, 16,* 56–64.

Fisher, D., Frey, N., & Lapp, D. (2012). *Text complexity: Raising rigor in reading.* Newark, DE: International Reading Association.

Fisher, D., Frey, N., & Pumpian, I. (2012). *How to create a culture of achievement in your school and classroom.* Alexandria, VA: Association for Supervision and Curriculum Development.

Fisher, D., Frey, N., & Rothenberg, C. (2011). *Implementing RTI with English learners.* Bloomington, IN: Solution Tree Press.

Fisher, D., Roach, V., & Frey, N. (2002). Examining the general programmatic benefits on inclusive schools. *International Journal of Inclusive Education, 6,* 63–78.

Frase, L. E. (1992). Constructive feedback on teaching is missing. *Education, 113*(2), 176–181.

Frey, N. (2006). The role of 1:1 individual instruction in reading. *Theory Into Practice, 45*(3), 207–214.

Frey, N., & Fisher, D. (2010). Getting to quality: A meeting of the minds. *Principal Leadership, 11*(1), 68–70.

Frey, N., & Fisher, D. (2011). *The formative assessment action plan: Practical steps to more successful teaching and learning.* Alexandria, VA: Association for Supervision and Curriculum Development.

Frey, N., Fisher, D., & Berkin, A. (2008). *Good habits, great readers: Building the literacy community.* Upper Saddle River, NJ: Allyn & Bacon.

Frey, N., Fisher, D., & Everlove, S. (2009). *Productive group work: How to engage students, build teamwork, and promote understanding.* Alexandria, VA: Association for Supervision and Curriculum Development.

Frey, N., Fisher, D., & Gonzalez, A. (2010). *Literacy 2.0: Reading and writing in the 21st century.* Bloomington, IN: Solution Tree Press.

Gamoran, S. (2007). *Standards-based reform and the poverty gap: Lessons from No Child Left Behind.* Washington, DC: Brookings Institution.

Gay, G. (2000). *Culturally responsive teaching: Theory, research, and practice* (Multicultural Education Series). New York: Teachers College Press.

Gentry, J. R. (2006). *Breaking the code: The science of beginning reading and writing.* Portsmouth, NH: Heinemann.

Gibbons, G. (1993). *From seed to plant.* New York: Holiday House.

Glickman, C. D., Gordon, S. P., & Ross-Gordon, J. M. (2004). *Supervision and instructional leadership: A developmental approach* (6th ed.). Boston: Allyn & Bacon.

Hallinger, P. (2003). Leading educational change: Reflection on the practices of instructional and transformational leadership. *Cambridge Journal of Education, 33*(3), 329–351.

Hallinger, P., Bickman, L., & Davis, K. (1996). School context, principal leadership, and student reading achievement. *The Elementary School Journal, 96*(5), 527–549.

Hallinger, P., & Heck, R. (1999). Next generation methods for the study of leadership and school improvement. In J. Murphy & K. S. Louis (Eds.), *Handbook of research on educational administration* (2nd ed., pp. 141–162). San Francisco: Jossey-Bass.

Halverson, R., Grigg, J., Prichett, R., & Thomas, C. (2007). The new instructional leadership: Creating data-driven instructional systems in school. *Journal of School Leadership, 17*(2), 159–194.

Hattie, J. (2009). *Visible learning: A synthesis of over 800 meta-analyses related to achievement.* New York: Routledge.

Hattie, J., & Timperley, H. (2007). The power of feedback. *Review of Educational Research, 77*, 81–112.

Heck, R. H. (1992). Principals' instructional leadership and school performance: Implications for policy development. *Educational Evaluation of Policy Analysis, 14*(1), 21–34.

Heck, R. H. (2000). Examining the impact of school quality on school outcomes and improvement: A value-added approach. *Educational Administration Quarterly, 36*(4), 513–552.

Heck, R. H., Larsen, T. J., & Marcoulides, G. A. (1990). Instructional leadership and school achievement: Validation of a causal model. *Educational Administration Quarterly, 26*(2), 92–125.

Herrell, A. L., & Jordan, M. (2011). *Fifty strategies for teaching English language learners* (4th ed.). Boston: Allyn & Bacon.

Hill, H. C., Kapitula, L., & Umland, K. (2011). A validity argument approach to evaluating teacher value-added scores. *American Educational Research Journal, 48*(3), 794–831.

Hinnant, J. B., O'Brien, M., & Ghazarian, S. R. (2009). The longitudinal relations of teacher expectations to achievement in the early school years. *Journal of Educational Psychology, 101*(3), 662–670.

Illinois ASPIRE. (2009). *Reading and response to intervention: Putting it all together.* Accessed at www.illinoisaspire.org/welcome/files/Reading_RtI_Guide.pdf on September 26, 2012.

Individuals With Disabilities Education Improvement Act, 20 U.S.C. § 1400 (2004).

Ing, M. (2009). Using informal classroom observations to improve instruction. *Journal of Educational Administration*, *48*(3), 337–358.

Johnson, J. F. (2002). High-performing, high-poverty, urban elementary schools. In P. D. Pearson & B. Taylor (Eds.), *Teaching reading: Effective schools, accomplished teachers* (pp. 89–114). Mahwah, NJ: Erlbaum.

Johnson, J. F., Jr., & Asera, R. (1999). *Hope for urban education: A study of nine high-performing, high-poverty, urban elementary schools*. Washington, DC: U.S. Department of Education.

Johnson, J. F., Lein, L., & Ragland, M. (1998). Highly successful schools in communities challenged by poverty. In Y. S. George & V. V. Van Horne (Eds.), *Science education reform for all (SERA): Sustaining the science, mathematics, and technology reform* (pp. 111–116). Washington, DC: American Association for the Advancement of Science.

Johnson, J. F., Uline, C. L., & Perez, L. (2011). Expert noticing and principals of high-performing urban schools. *Journal of Education for Students Placed at Risk*, *16*(2), 122–136.

Joyce, B., & Showers, B. (1983). *Power in staff development through research on training*. Washington, DC: Association for Supervision and Curriculum Development.

Kanevsky, L., & Keighley, T. (2003). To produce or not to produce? Understanding boredom and the honor in underachievement. *Roeper Review*, *26*(1), 20–28.

Kluth, P., & Darmody-Latham, J. (2003). Beyond sight words: Literacy opportunities for students with autism. *The Reading Teacher*, *56*(6), 532–535.

Krashen, S. D. (1985). *The input hypothesis: Issues and implications*. New York: Longman.

Lapp, D., Fisher, D., Flood, J., & Cabello, A. (2001). An integrated approach to the teaching and assessment of language arts. In S. R. Hurley & J. V. Tinajero (Eds.), *Literacy assessment of second language learners* (pp. 1–26). Needham Heights, MA: Allyn & Bacon.

Lee, J., & Reeves, T. (2012). Revisiting the impact of NCLB high-stakes accountability, capacity, and resources: State NAEP 1990–2009 reading and mathematics achievement trends. *Educational Evaluation and Policy Analysis*, *34*(2), 209–231.

Leithwood, K. (2005). Understanding successful principal leadership: Progress on a broken front. *Journal of Educational Administration*, *43*(6), 619–629.

Leithwood, K., & Jantzi, D. (1999). Transformational school leadership effects: A replication. *School Effectiveness and School Improvement*, *10*(4), 451–479.

Leithwood, K., Louis, K. S., Anderson, S., & Wahlstrom, K. (2004). *How leadership influences student learning.* Toronto, ON: Center for Applied Research and Educational Improvement, Ontario Institute for Studies in Education.

Leithwood, K., & Riehl, C. (2005). What we know about successful school leadership. In W. Firestone & C. Riehl (Eds.), *A new agenda: Directions for research on educational leadership* (Critical Issues in Educational Leadership, pp. 22–47). New York: Teachers College Press.

Leithwood, K., & Sun, J. (2012). The nature and effects of transformational school leadership: A meta-analytic review of unpublished research. *Educational Administration Quarterly, 48,* 387–423.

Louis, K. S., Marks, H. M., & Kruse, S. (1996). Teachers' professional community in restructuring schools. *American Educational Research Journal, 33,* 757–798.

Maden, M. (2001). *Success against the odds, five years on: Revisiting effective schools in disadvantaged areas.* London: RoutledgeFalmer.

Mallery, J. L., & Mallery, J. G. (1999). The American legacy of ability grouping: Tracking reconsidered. *Multicultural Education, 7,* 13–15.

Mangin, M. (2007). Facilitating elementary principals' support for instructional teacher leadership. *Educational Administration Quarterly, 43*(3), 319–357.

Marks, H., & Printy, S. (2003). Principal leadership and school performance: An integration of transformational and instructional leadership. *Educational Administration Quarterly, 39*(3), 370–397.

Michaels, S., O'Connor, C., & Resnick, L. (2008). Deliberative discourse idealized and realized: Accountable Talk in the classroom and in civic life. *Studies in Philosophy and Education, 27*(4), 283–297.

Moll, L. C., Amanti, C., Neff, D., & González, N. (1992). Funds of knowledge for teaching: Using a qualitative approach to connect homes and classrooms. *Theory Into Practice, 31*(1), 132–141.

Moss, B. (2005). Making a case and a place for effective content area literacy instruction in the elementary grades. *The Reading Teacher, 59*(1), 46–55.

Mullen, C. A., & Hutinger, J. L. (2008). The principal's role in fostering collaborative learning communities through faculty study group development. *Theory Into Practice, 47,* 276–285.

Murphy, J., Elliot, S. N., Goldring, E., & Porter, A. C. (2007). Leadership for learning: A research-based model and taxonomy of behaviors. *School Leadership and Management, 27*(2), 179–201.

National Education Goals Panel. (1998). *Ready schools.* Washington, DC: Author.

National Governors Association Center for Best Practices & Council of Chief State School Officers. (2010a). *Common Core State Standards for English language arts and literacy in history/social science, science, & technical subjects.* Washington, DC: Authors. Accessed at www.corestandards.org/assets /CCSSI_ELA%20Standards.pdf on September 26, 2012.

National Governors Association Center for Best Practices & Council of Chief State School Officers. (2010b). *Common Core State Standards for English language arts and literacy in history/social science, science, & technical subjects: Appendix A—Research supporting key elements of the standards.* Washington, DC: Authors. Accessed at www.corestandards.org/assets/Appendix_A.pdf on September 26, 2012.

National Governors Association Center for Best Practices & Council of Chief State School Officers. (2010c). *Common Core State Standards for English language arts and literacy in history/social science, science, & technical subjects: Appendix B—Text exemplars and sample performance tasks.* Washington, DC: Authors. Accessed at www.corestandards.org/assets/Appendix_B.pdf on September 26, 2012.

National Institute of Child Health and Human Development. (2000). *Report of the National Reading Panel: Teaching children to read—An evidence-based assessment of the scientific research literature on reading and its implications for reading instruction* (NIH Publication No. 00-4769). Washington, DC: U.S. Government Printing Office.

Navan, J. L. (2002). Enhancing the achievement of "all" learners means high ability students too. *Middle School Journal, 34*(2), 45–49.

Nelson, B. S., & Sassi, A. (2000). Shifting approaches to supervision: The case of mathematics supervision. *Educational Administration Quarterly, 36*(4), 553–584.

No Child Left Behind Act of 2001, 20 U.S.C. § 6319 (2008).

Olivier, D. F., & Hipp, K. K. (2006). Leadership capacity and collective efficacy: Interacting to sustain student learning in a professional learning community. *Journal of School Leadership, 16*(5), 505–519.

Paris, S. G. (2005). Reinterpreting the development of reading skills. *Reading Research Quarterly, 40*(2), 184–202.

Pearson, P. D., & Gallagher, G. (1983). The gradual release of responsibility model of instruction. *Contemporary Educational Psychology, 8,* 112–123.

Perez, L. G., & Uline, C. (2003). Educational administrative problem solving in the Information Age: Building and employing technological capacity. *Journal of Educational Administration, 41*(2), 143–157.

Piaget, J. (1952). *The origins of intelligence in children.* New York: Norton.

Putnam, R. T., & Borko, H. (1997). Teacher learning: Implications of new views of cognition. In B. J. Biddle, T. L. Good, & I. F. Goodson (Eds.), *The international handbook of teachers and teaching: Rethinking goals and approaches* (pp. 1223–1296). Dordrecht, the Netherlands: Kluwer.

Rasinski, T. (2011). The art and science of teaching reading fluency. In D. Lapp & D. Fisher (Eds.), *Handbook of research in teaching the English language arts: Co-sponsored by the International Reading Association and the National Council of Teachers of English* (3rd ed., pp. 238–246). New York: Routledge.

Reeves, D. (2005). Putting it all together: Standards, assessment, and accountability in successful professional learning communities. In R. DuFour, R. Eaker, & R. DuFour (Eds.), *On common ground: The power of professional learning communities* (pp. 45–63). Bloomington, IN: Solution Tree Press.

Reitzug, U. C. (1997). Images of principal instructional leadership: From supervision to collaborative inquiry. *Journal of Curriculum and Supervision, 12*(4), 356–366.

Reschly, A. (2010). *Schools, families, and response to intervention.* Washington, DC: RTI Action Network. Accessed at www.rtinetwork.org/essential/family/schools-familes-and-rti on December 14, 2012.

Robinson, V. M. J., Lloyd, C. A., & Rowe, K. J. (2008). The impact of leadership on student outcomes: An analysis of the differential effects of leadership types. *Educational Administration Quarterly, 44*(5), 635–674.

Ryndak, D. L., Morrison, A. P., & Sommerstein, L. (1999). Literacy before and after inclusion in general education settings: A case study. *Journal of the Association for Persons with Severe Handicaps, 24*(1), 5–22.

Scheurich, J. J. (1998). Highly successful and loving, public elementary schools populated mainly by low-SES children of color: Core beliefs and cultural characteristics. *Urban Education, 33*(4), 451–491.

Schmar-Dobler, E. (2003). Reading on the Internet: The link between literacy and technology. *Journal of Adolescent and Adult Literacy, 47*(1), 80–85.

Sciarra, D. T., & Ambrosino, K. E. (2011). Post-secondary expectations and educational attainment. *Professional School Counseling, 14*(3), 231–241.

Sheppard, B. (1996). Exploring the transformational nature of instructional leadership. *Alberta Journal of Educational Research, 42*(4), 325–344.

Slavin, R. E., & Braddock, J. H., III (1993). Ability grouping: On the wrong track. *College Board Review, 168*, 11–17.

Slotnik, W. J. (2010). The buck stops here: Tying what students learn to what educators earn. *Phi Delta Kappan, 91*(8), 44–48.

Snell, M. E., & Janney, R. (2006). *Social relationships and peer support* (2nd ed.). Baltimore: Brookes.

Stiggins, R. J. (2001). The unfulfilled promise of classroom assessment. *Educational Measurement: Issues and Practice, 20*(3), 5–14.

Stoll, L., Bolam, R., McMahon, A., Wallace, M., & Thomas, S. (2006). Professional learning communities: A review of the literature. *Journal of Educational Change, 7*(4), 221–258.

Suárez-Orozco, C., Suárez-Orozco, M. M., & Todorova, I. (2008). *Learning a new land: Immigrant students in American society.* Cambridge, MA: Harvard University Press.

Supovitz, J. A., & Riggan, M. (2012). *Building a foundation for school leadership: An evaluation of the Annenberg Distributed Leadership project, 2006–2010.* Philadelphia: Consortium for Policy Research in Education. Accessed at http://cpre.org/sites/default/files/researchreport/1346_1299cpre-1003dlrrfinal .pdf on December 10, 2012.

Supovitz, J. A., Sirinides, P., & May, H. (2010). How principals and peers influence teaching and learning. *Educational Administration Quarterly, 46*(1), 31–56.

Thousand, J. S., Villa, R. A., & Nevin, A. I. (Eds.). (2002). *Creativity and collaborative learning: The practical guide to empowering students, teachers, and families* (2nd ed.). Baltimore: Brookes.

Toulmin, S. (1958). *The uses of argument.* Cambridge, England: Cambridge University Press.

Uline, C. (1997). School architecture as a subject of inquiry. *The Journal of School Leadership, 7*(2), 194–209.

Uline, C., Tschannen-Moran, M., & Perez, L. (2003). Constructive conflict: How controversy contributes to school improvement. *Teachers College Record, 105*(5), 782–816.

U.S. Department of Education, Office of Intergovernmental and Interagency Affairs, Educational Partnerships and Family Involvement Unit. (2003). *Reading tips for parents.* Washington, DC: Author.

Vaughn, S., & Fletcher, J. M. (2012). Response to intervention with secondary school students with reading difficulties. *Journal of Learning Disabilities, 45*(3), 244–256.

Vaughn, S., & Linan-Thompson, S. (2003). Group size and time allotted to intervention: Effects for students with reading difficulties. In B. R. Foorman (Ed.), *Preventing and remediating reading difficulties: Bringing science to scale* (pp. 299–324). Baltimore: York.

Vygotsky, L. S. (1962). *Thought and language.* Cambridge, MA: MIT Press.

Vygotsky, L. S. (1978). *Mind in society: The development of higher psychological processes.* Cambridge, MA: Harvard University Press.

Wanzek, J., & Vaughn, S. (2010). Tier 3 interventions for students with significant reading problems. *Theory Into Practice, 49*(4), 305–314.

Waters, J. T., Marzano, R. J., & McNulty, B. A. (2003). *Balanced leadership: What 30 years of research tells us about the effect of leadership on student achievement.* Aurora, CO: Mid-Continent Research for Education and Learning.

Wood, D., Bruner, J. S., & Ross, G. (1976). The role of tutoring and problem solving. *Journal of Child Psychology and Psychiatry, 17,* 89–100.

Yovanoff, P., Duesbery, L., & Alonzo, J. (2005). Grade-level invariance of a theoretical causal structure predicting reading comprehension with vocabulary and oral language fluency. *Educational Measurement: Issues & Practices, 24*(3), 4–12.

Zatynski, M. (2012). Revamping teacher evaluation. *Principal, 91*(5), 22–27.

INDEX

Other books in the *Common Core English Language Arts in a PLC at Work™* series:

Common Core English Language Arts in a PLC at Work™, Grades K–2 by Douglas Fisher and Nancy Frey
BKF580

Common Core English Language Arts in a PLC at Work™, Grades 3–5 by Douglas Fisher and Nancy Frey
BKF582

Common Core English Language Arts in a PLC at Work™, Grades 6–8 by Douglas Fisher and Nancy Frey
BKF584

Common Core English Language Arts in a PLC at Work™, Grades 9–12 by Douglas Fisher and Nancy Frey
BKF586

Teaching Students to Read Like Detectives
Douglas Fisher, Nancy Frey, and Diane Lapp

Prompt students to become the sophisticated readers, writers, and thinkers they need to be to achieve higher learning. Explore the important relationship between text, learner, and learning, and gain an array of methods to establish critical literacy in a discussion-based and reflective classroom.
BKF499

How to Teach Thinking Skills Within the Common Core
James A. Bellanca, Robin J. Fogarty, and Brian M. Pete

Empower your students to thrive across the curriculum. Packed with examples and tools, this practical guide prepares teachers across all grade levels and content areas to teach the most critical cognitive skills from the Common Core State Standards.
BKF576

20 Literacy Strategies to Meet the Common Core
Elaine K. McEwan-Adkins and Allyson J. Burnett

With the advent of the Common Core State Standards, some secondary teachers are scrambling for what to do and how to do it. This book provides twenty research-based strategies designed to help students meet those standards and become expert readers.
BKF588

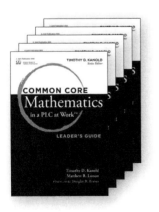

Common Core Mathematics in a PLC at Work™ Series
Edited by Timothy D. Kanold

These teacher guides illustrate how to sustain successful implementation of the Common Core State Standards for Mathematics. Discover what students should learn and how they should learn it at each grade level. Comprehensive and research-affirmed analysis tools and strategies will help you and your collaborative team develop and assess student demonstrations of deep conceptual understanding *and* procedural fluency.
Joint Publications With the National Council of Teachers of Mathematics
BKF566, BKF568, BKF574, BKF561, BKF559

Wait! Your professional development journey doesn't have to end with the last pages of this book.

We realize improving student learning doesn't happen overnight. And your school or district shouldn't be left to puzzle out all the details of this process alone.

No matter where you are on the journey, we're committed to helping you get to the next stage.

Take advantage of everything from **custom workshops** to **keynote presentations** and **interactive web and video conferencing**. We can even help you develop an action plan tailored to fit your specific needs.

Let's get the conversation started.

Call 888.763.9045 today.

 solution-tree.com

Solution Tree

Solution Tree's mission is to advance the work of our authors. By working with the best researchers and educators worldwide, we strive to be the premier provider of innovative publishing, in-demand events, and inspired professional development designed to transform education to ensure that all students learn.

The mission of the International Reading Association is to promote reading by continuously advancing the quality of literacy instruction and research worldwide.